ESSENTIAL
SAT
VOCABULARY
2024 - 2025

- Volume 1 -

The Most Effective
SAT STRATEGY

- LEARNING Through SHORT STORIES -

to Bonnie M.

- Dex Saunier

The Essential SAT Vocabulary 2024 – 2025 Vol. 1 features **750 words+** - and their associated synonyms - **commonly appearing during the SAT test**. This book is a complementary addition to your SAT preparation, by actively facilitating your memory retention in a different and more relaxed way.

To contact the author, write at contact@DexSaunier.com

Original Essential SAT Vocabulary 2024 – 2025 Vol. 1
A Dex Saunier Classic

ISBN: 979 - 8397704861

HOW TO USE YOUR
ESSENTIAL SAT 2024 – 2025 VOCABULARY BUILDER

SAT WORD → **Vacuous**

READ THE SHORT STORY

Because of intellectual pursuits, a vacuous mind stands as an unfilled vessel, devoid of depth and substance. It is a barren landscape where ideas fail to take root, leaving an echoing void. As a singular individual, lacking in curiosity and intellectual vigor, she drifts aimlessly through life, never seizing the boundless opportunities that await.

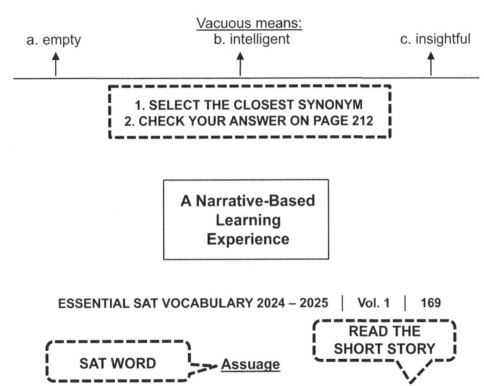

Vacuous means:

a. empty   b. intelligent   c. insightful

1. SELECT THE CLOSEST SYNONYM
2. CHECK YOUR ANSWER ON PAGE 212

A Narrative-Based Learning Experience

SAT WORD → **Assuage**

READ THE SHORT STORY

In the face of emotional turmoil and psychological distress, individuals yearn for solace and a means to assuage their inner pain. Compassionate support, gentle reassurance, and empathetic understanding can serve as an antidote for their wounded souls. By extending a helping hand and creating a nurturing environment, one can assist in alleviating suffering and fostering a sense of peace.

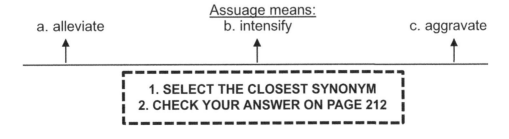

Assuage means:

a. alleviate   b. intensify   c. aggravate

1. SELECT THE CLOSEST SYNONYM
2. CHECK YOUR ANSWER ON PAGE 212

HOW TO USE YOUR
ESSENTIAL SAT 2024 – 2025 VOCABULARY BUILDER
Volume 1

> **Explore 750+ SAT Words Synonyms**
> **2,250 Synonyms Listed**

Turpitude : depravity, wickedness, corruption
Tyro : novice, beginner, neophyte
Ubiquitous : omnipresent, pervasive, universal
Unalloyed : pure, undiluted, genuine
Unctuous : oily, slick, sycophantic
Undermined : weaken, sabotage, subvert
Underscore : emphasize, highlight, accentuate
Unequivocal : clear, definite, unambiguous
Unfetter : liberate, free, release
Unfrock : defrock, dethrone, depose
Unprecedented : unparalleled, extraordinary, novel
Unscathed : unharmed, undamaged, intact
Unwitting : unaware, ignorant, unconscious
Upbraid : scold, reprimand, criticize
Uproarious : hilarious, boisterous, riotous

Immerse	yourself in 750 Short Stories
Master	750+ SAT Vocabulary Words
Explore	2,250 SAT Words Synonyms

> **Validate 750+ Unique Solutions**
> **Each SAT Word has a Unique Solution**

Page 167: Verbose: a – Assiduous: a – Cogent: b – Divert: a
Page 168: Fractious: b – Inscrutable: a – Mettle: a – Pellucid: a
Page 169: Punctilious: b – Spurious: a – Verbosity: a – Assuage: a
Page 170: Cogitate: a – Docile: c – Fraudulent: a – Insentient: c
Page 171: Milieu: a – Pensive: b – Purloin: a – Stagnant: b
Page 172: Vertigo: a – Astute: c – Collage: a – Dogmatic: a
Page 173: Frivolous: a – Insipid: b – Mire: a – Penury: a
Page 174: Pusillanimous: b – Staid: a – Vestigial: b – Asylum: a
Page 175: Collate: c – Dolt: b – Frugal: a – Instigate: b
Page 176: Misanthrope: c – Perceptive: a – Pyromania: a – Stanza: a
Page 177: Vignette: b – Atheist: a – Colloquial: a – Dotard: a
Page 178: Furrow: b – Instigator: a – Misnomer: a – Percipient: a
Page 179: Quaff: a – Staunch: c – Vilification: c – Atrophy: a

CONTENTS

ESSENTIAL SAT VOCABULARY 2024 - 2025
Volume 1

THE ESSENTIALS

THE MORE

Abhor

Amidst the vibrant bustle of the city, a young artist passionately immersed herself in the creation of her masterpiece. Her nimble fingers danced across the canvas, bringing to life a scene of breathtaking beauty. As she meticulously added the final strokes of color, a feeling of abhorrence emerged within her, contrasting the serenity of her artwork.

Abhor means:

a. despise   b. adore   c. admire

Bigot

In a diverse society, acceptance and understanding are fundamental values to embrace. However, there are individuals who stubbornly cling to their prejudiced beliefs. The narrow-mindedness of a bigot can create division and hinder progress, undermining the very essence of unity and equality.

Bigot means:

a. tolerant   b. inclusive   c. racist

Counterfeit

The undercover investigator meticulously examined the intricate details of the suspicious artwork. Through her trained eye, she could discern the subtle discrepancies that betrayed its authenticity. It was a crafty attempt to deceive, a counterfeit creation that aimed to deceive unsuspecting art collectors.

Counterfeit means:

a. forged   b. genuine   c. original

Enfranchise

In the pursuit of democracy, suffrage was a hard-fought battle, granting equal rights and representation for all citizens. The decision to enfranchise every eligible individual irrespective of their race, gender, or social status marked a significant milestone in the path towards equality. It grant rights to the voice of the people, ensuring a fair and inclusive democratic process.

Enfranchise means:

a. empower   b. suppress   c. deprive

Hamper

As the marathon runner reached the final stretch of the race, fatigue began to take its toll on her weary legs. The blisters and aching muscles threatened to hamper her progress, but her determination propelled her forward. With sheer willpower, she pushed through the physical limitations, crossing the finish line triumphantly.

Hamper means:

a. facilitate   b. hinder   c. aid

Kindle

In the dead of winter, as the snow blanketed the landscape, a group of friends gathered around the crackling bonfire. The dancing flames cast a warm glow, kindling a sense of camaraderie and storytelling. As the night wore on, the fire's radiant heat and captivating stories ignited a sense of nostalgia and friendship among the group.

Kindle means:

a. arouse   b. dampen   c. suppress

Noxious

The serene garden was a haven of tranquility, with its colorful blossoms swaying in the gentle breeze. Bees buzzed harmoniously, collecting nectar from the fragrant flowers. However, hidden among the petals lurked a noxious presence, releasing toxic fumes that disrupted the harmony of the peaceful sanctuary.

Noxious means:

a. safe   b. benign   c. toxic

Placid

The sun's golden rays draped the tranquil lake in a soothing glow, reflecting the serene beauty of the surrounding landscape. With each gentle ripple on the water's surface, the placid scene emanated a sense of blissful calm. Nature's symphony accompanied the serenity, inviting all to embrace the peaceful respite.

Placid means:

a. chaotic   b. calm   c. restless

Remuneration

After years of tireless dedication and unwavering commitment to her craft, the talented artist received the recognition she deserved. The applause filled the grand theater as the audience acknowledged her remarkable talent, applauding with heartfelt admiration. With tears of joy, she gracefully accepted the remuneration for her invaluable contribution to the art world.

Remuneration means:

a. penalty   b. reward   c. deprivation

Talisman

In a mystical realm of forgotten legends, a brave warrior embarked on a treacherous journey to retrieve a powerful artifact. Legends spoke of a talisman said to grant its possessor invincibility and unimaginable strength. With unwavering determination, the warrior overcame countless trials, ultimately claiming the talisman as his own.

Talisman means:

a. hex   b. curse   c. charm

Abrasive

The sculptor meticulously chiseled away at the rough stone, transforming it into a work of art. Every stroke of the abrasive tool brought forth intricate details, revealing the hidden beauty within. With precision and patience, the sculptor created a masterpiece that captured the essence of elegance and grace.

Abrasive means:

a. rough   b. smooth   c. delicate

Bilk

In a world where trust can be fragile, a cunning swindler sought to deceive the unsuspecting victims by weaving an intricate web of lies. With charming charisma, the con artist bilked countless individuals, leaving them empty-handed and disillusioned. However, justice prevailed when the truth was unveiled, and the swindler faced the consequences of their deceit.

Bilk means:

a. reimburse   b. defraud   c. refund

Covert

Under the moonlit sky, a group of skilled operatives embarked on a mission of utmost secrecy. Their mission was to retrieve a confidential document from a heavily guarded facility without arousing suspicion. With meticulous planning and unwavering determination, they successfully infiltrated the covert operation, leaving no trace of their presence.

Covert means:

a. obvious   b. hidden   c. visible

Engender

In the wake of a devastating natural disaster, the resilient community came together, united by a shared sense of purpose and determination. The challenging circumstances engendered a spirit of compassion and empathy among the people, fostering a supportive environment where everyone lent a helping hand. Through collective effort, they triumphed over adversity and emerged stronger than ever.

Engender means:

a. stifle   b. quell   c. generate

Hangar

The colossal aircraft gracefully descended from the endless sky, finding its temporary sanctuary within the fortified hangar. Standing tall, the hangar was a colossal structure capable of sheltering multiple aircraft, ensuring their protection from the elements. Within its steel embrace, the aircraft underwent meticulous maintenance and preparation before embarking on their next aerial journey.

Hangar means:

a. exposed   b. depot   c. open

Knotty

As the gifted mathematician delved into the complex problem, she encountered a series of knotty equations that tested the limits of her intellect. The complex web of numbers and variables challenged her logical reasoning, but her unwavering determination fueled her resolve to unravel the powerful knot. Through meticulous analysis and innovative strategies, she untangled the complex puzzle and unveiled a groundbreaking mathematical breakthrough.

Knotty means:

a. easy   b. intricate   c. simple

Nuance

In the art's world, the master painter delicately blended vibrant hues, skillfully infusing each stroke with subtle nuances of shade and tone. These nuanced variations brought depth and complexity to the canvas, evoking a range of emotions within the observer. With an astute eye for detail, the painter created a masterpiece that transcended the boundaries of ordinary perception.

Nuance means:

a. clarity   b. refinement   c. simplicity

Plagiarism

In academia, integrity and originality were paramount virtues that scholars were expected to uphold. Plagiarism, the act of fraudulently presenting someone else's work as one's own, was vehemently condemned and regarded as a grave offense. The consequences of plagiarizing another's ideas ranged from tarnishing one's reputation to severe academic repercussions.

Plagiarism means:

a. innovation   b. piracy   c. originality

Renown

In a bustling city filled with aspiring musicians, one exceptional violinist stood out from the rest. With each soul-stirring melody composed, her talent garnered admiration and respect from both the audience and her fellow musicians. Her musical prowess and dedication brought her the renown she deserved.

Renown means:

a. fame   b. notoriety   c. anonymity

Tangent

The brilliant mathematician's mind was always abuzz with numerous intellectual pursuits. During a conversation about astronomy, he suddenly veered off on a tangent, discussing the intricate patterns of fractals and their significance in chaos theory. Even though his divergent thinking sometimes confused those around him, it was on these tangents that he often made groundbreaking discoveries.

Tangent means:

a. relevance   b. digression   c. directness

Abasement

In the pursuit of power, the tyrant resorted to tactics of abasement, deliberately demeaning and humiliating those who opposed him. Through this strategy, he aimed to undermine their confidence and assert his dominance. However, he failed to recognize that true strength lies in mutual respect and collaboration, not in the abasement of others.

Abasement means:

a. dignity   b. humiliation   c. pride

Billowing

The storm clouds loomed ominously in the distance, causing the once clear sky to darken. As the winds picked up speed, the sea surged and the waves grew higher, billowing ferociously against the rugged cliffs. Nature's power was on display, unveiling its might through the tumbling force of the tempestuous storm.

Billowing means:

a. surging   b. stagnant   c. motionless

Cower

In a world plagued by injustice, the oppressed population lived in constant fear, their spirits crushed by the ruthless regimes that ruled over them. With bowed heads and downcast eyes, they cowered, trembling beneath the weight of tyranny. But little did their oppressors know that this act of cowering only fueled their determination to rise and reclaim their rights.

Cower means:

a. cringe   b. face   c. challenge

Enhance

The skilled photographer meticulously adjusted the settings on his camera, aiming to enhance the natural beauty of the landscape before him. With each click of the shutter, he captured the vibrant colors and intricate details that were often overlooked by the naked eye. The final result was a collection of breathtaking photographs that showcased the incredible splendor of nature.

Enhance means:

a. improve   b. weaken   c. impair

Harangue

The passionate activist, known for her eloquence and fierce determination, took the stage and embarked on a passionate speech, fervently addressing the grievances faced by marginalized communities. She appealed to the audience's sense of justice and called for immediate action to rectify the injustices that prevailed. Her powerful harangue left an indelible impact, igniting a spark of change in the hearts of those who listened.

Harangue means:

a. praise   b. compliment   c. diatribe

Labyrinth

Deep within the heart of an ancient castle lay a labyrinth, its intricate pathways shrouded in mystery and whispers of forgotten legends. Many had attempted to navigate its bewildering corridors, but only a select few had managed to unlock its secrets and emerge victorious. Legends spoke of a treasure hidden within the labyrinth, waiting to be discovered by those who possessed both cunning and courage.

Labyrinth means:

a. maze   b. direct   c. straightforward

Nullify

When faced with an unlawful action, the court had the power to nullify the unjust decision, ensuring justice prevailed. The judge meticulously examined the evidence presented, seeking any legal loopholes or errors that could void the ruling. In the end, the court determined that the defendant's constitutional rights had been violated, leading them to annul the verdict.

Nullify means:

a. validate   b. invalidate   c. affirm

Plaintiff

In the grand courtroom, the plaintiff, a brave survivor, took the stand, ready to tell her story and seek justice against those who had wronged her. With unwavering composure, she recounted the harrowing experiences that had forever changed her life, leaving the audience captivated by her courage and resilience. Her voice echoed through the halls of justice, demanding accountability and reparations.

Plaintiff means:

a. defendant   b. respondent   c. accuser

Replete

The opulent banquet hall was replete with a decadent array of delicacies from around the world, enticing the guests with their enticing aromas and exquisite presentations. The tables overflowed with platters of gourmet cuisine, each dish meticulously crafted to satiate even the most discerning palate. As the guests indulged in the sumptuous feast, their senses were overwhelmed by the abundance and richness of the offerings.

Replete means:

    a. full   b. empty   c. sparse

Tangible

The artist's creativity knew no bounds as she transformed her visions into tangible works of art, breathing life into her imagination through her skilled hands. Using a myriad of mediums, she crafted sculptures that seemed to transcend reality, evoking emotions within those who beheld them. The incredible beauty of her creations served as a testament to the limitless possibilities that art could manifest.

Tangible means:

    a. elusive   b. palpable   c. evasive

Abrogate

In a world governed by law and order, the parliament held a crucial vote to abrogate an outdated statute that stifled individual freedoms. The lawmakers engaged in spirited debates, analyzing the legal ramifications and social implications of this momentous decision. Finally, with an overwhelming majority, they resolved to abolish the archaic law, heralding a new era of progress and equality.

Abrogate means:

    a. revoke   b. establish   c. preserve

Blasphemy

Within the hallowed halls of the church, the clergy preached about the sanctity of faith and the sacred tenets that shaped their beliefs. Any act or utterance that defied these revered principles was considered blasphemy, a direct affront to the divine. The faithful congregation sought solace in their devotion, shielding themselves from the profanity that threatened to undermine their spiritual sanctuary.

Blasphemy means:

    a. reverence   b. heresy   c. piety

Credible

In journalism, the pursuit of truth is paramount, and only credible sources are relied upon to report the news. Seasoned reporters meticulously corroborate facts with multiple independent witnesses, ensuring the veracity of their stories. With the rise of fake news, the need for credible journalism become even more crucial in order to distinguish fact from fiction.

Credible means:

a. dubious
b. reliable
c. questionable

Enigma

The secrets that shrouded the eccentric billionaire intrigued the world, as countless speculations arose about the origins of his vast fortune. He had mastered the art of mystique, revealing little about his past and keeping his intentions hidden beneath a veil of secrecy. Journalists and historians alike endeavored to unravel the enigma that surrounded this enigmatic figure, yearning to uncover the truth.

Enigma means:

a. clarity
b. transparency
c. mystery

Harbingers

As the first rays of dawn pierced through the darkness, the melodious songs of the birds resonated in perfect harmony, serving as harbingers of a new day. Nature celebrated this transition, as flowers bloomed and the gentle breeze whispered promises of hope. The harbingers of spring brought a renewal of life, casting away the frigid grip of winter.

Harbingers means:

a. indicators
b. deniers
c. suppressors

Labyrinthine

The ancient temple concealed within its labyrinthine structure the wisdom and secrets of generations past. Curious explorers ventured deep into its dimly lit corridors, their steps guided only by torchlight and a thirst for knowledge. Each twist and turn presented new challenges, and only those with an unwavering determination could hope to navigate through the complex path to enlightenment.

Labyrinthine means:

a. intricate
b. uncomplicated
c. direct

Nuzzle

The elderly couple sat on the porch, reminiscing about their youthful adventures and the tender moments they shared. With a playful glint in his eye, the husband leaned in to nuzzle his wife's cheek, their love bridging the gap between the past and the present, symbolizing the enduring bond they had nurtured over the years.

Nuzzle means:

a. cuddle　　　　　b. separate　　　　　c. repel

Plaudit

The theater erupted in thunderous applause as the curtains fell, signaling the end of the breathtaking performance. The audience, captivated by the actors' impeccable skills and the mesmerizing set design, showered them with plaudits, a testament to their talent and dedication to their craft.

Plaudit means:

a. acclaim　　　　　b. censure　　　　　c. criticism

Reprehensible

The heinous act committed by the criminal was undeniably reprehensible, with its repercussions reverberating throughout the community. The citizens, fueled by a collective sense of justice, called for swift action to ensure that such vicious behavior would never be tolerated in their midst.

Reprehensible means:

a. admirable　　　　　b. virtuous　　　　　c. immoral

Tardy

The diligent student, known for her punctuality and commitment to her studies, was alarmed to find herself tardy for the final exam. Despite her best efforts to arrive on time, unforeseen circumstances had conspired against her. With a heavy heart, she entered the classroom, hoping it wouldn't mar her academic record.

Tardy means:

a. late　　　　　b. prompt　　　　　c. early

Absolution

The remorseful sinner knelt before the clergy, seeking absolution for the mistakes and transgressions that burdened his conscience. The priest, with wisdom and compassion in his eyes, offered words of kindness and redemption, granting the repentant soul the absolution he so desperately sought.

Absolution means:

a. guilt   b. blame   c. forgiveness

Blatant

The politician's blatant disregard for ethical standards and strident manipulation of facts drew widespread criticism from the public. The citizens, disillusioned by corruption and deceit, demanded transparency and integrity in their elected officials, vowing to hold them accountable for their actions.

Blatant means:

a. evident   b. discreet   c. subtle

Creditable

The young scientist worked tirelessly in her laboratory, conducting experiments and analyzing data in pursuit of a breakthrough in renewable energy. Her meticulous research and unwavering dedication were nothing short of creditable, positioning her as a rising star in the scientific community.

Creditable means:

a. reputable   b. unworthy   c. discreditable

Ensconce

The weary traveler, exhausted from a long journey, sought refuge in a quaint inn nestled amidst rolling hills. As he entered his cozy room, he couldn't help but feel a sense of comfort and security, ensconced from the bustling world outside.

Ensconce means:

a. settle   b. expose   c. reveal

Hasten

With time running out and the deadline looming, the team of engineers had to hasten their efforts to complete the ambitious construction project. They worked day and night, fueled by a sense of urgency and determination, striving to overcome every obstacle that stood in their way.

Hasten means:

a. accelerate b. hinder c. delay

Laceration

The courageous firefighter, battling the raging inferno, emerged from the burning building with a deep laceration on his arm. Despite the pain and bloodshed, his unwavering resolve never wavered as he continued to save lives and protect the community from the devastating blaze.

Laceration means:

a. gash b. closure c. mend

Obdurate

The stubborn dictator remained obdurate in the face of widespread protests and international pressure, refusing to heed the cries for democracy and human rights. His unyielding stance led to further unrest and division within the country, leaving the citizens disillusioned and yearning for change.

Obdurate means:

a. flexible b. yielding c. resolute

Plausible

As the detective pieced together the clues and evidence, a plausible theory about the crime began to emerge. The intricate web of motives and alibis seemed to align, pointing towards a suspect whose guilt became increasingly realistic with each new revelation.

Plausible means:

a. credible b. unrealistic c. incredible

Reprieve

In the depths of despair, the condemned prisoner received an unexpected relief, a glimmer of hope amidst the darkness of their impending fate. The announcement of a temporary stay of execution breathed new life into their weary soul, granting them a brief respite from the clutches of death. As the reprieve was granted, the prisoner felt a surge of gratitude, longing to embrace the second chance that had been bestowed upon them.

Reprieve means:

a. pardon   b. sentence   c. penalty

Tawdry

The aspiring fashion designer showcased a collection of garments that exuded a tawdry glamour, bedazzled with gaudy sequins and glittering beads. Their ostentatious designs seemed to defy the principles of elegance and sophistication, favoring a cheap allure that left many critics perplexed. Although some may argue that beauty can be found in the unconventional, the vulgar creations failed to capture the essence of true style.

Tawdry means:

a. tacky   b. elegant   c. classy

Abstain

In the face of relentless peer pressure, the young individual possessed the strength of character to abstain from partaking in harmful vices that engulfed their social circle. Resolute in his decision, he held steadfast to his principles, refusing to succumb to the temptation that surrounded him. Through his choice to abstain, he became an exemplar of self-restraint and a source of inspiration for others in similar circumstances.

Abstain means:

a. indulge   b. avoid   c. embrace

Blighted

The once flourishing town had fallen into a state of utter desolation, its vibrant streets now blighted by dilapidated buildings and pervasive poverty. The sense of hope that once permeated the community had withered away, replaced by a pervasive sense of despair. Despite the conditions that encased the town, small pockets of resilience and determination remained, a testament to the indomitable spirit of its inhabitants.

Blighted means:

a. ruined   b. thriving   c. prosperous

Credulous

The charlatan preyed upon the credulous nature of unsuspecting individuals, weaving tales of grandeur and false promises that ensnared their vulnerable minds. Exploiting their gullibility and readiness to believe, the con artist swindled fortunes from those who placed blind trust in their persuasive words. It was only when the victims realized the extent of their credulous nature that they vowed to become more discerning and skeptical.

Credulous means:

a. skeptical   b. naive   c. suspicious

Enshroud

As night fell upon the ancient cemetery, a thick mist enshrouded the gravestones, veiling the site in an eerie cloak of darkness. Shadows danced among the tombstones, their ominous presence heightening the sense of unease in the graveyard. The ethereal fog covered every corner, lending an air of mystery and an unsettling atmosphere to the sacred resting place of the deceased.

Enshroud means:

a. reveal   b. cloak   c. illuminate

Haughtiness

The acclaimed professor, renowned for his vast knowledge and intellectual prowess, lectured with an air of confidence and superiority. His erudite discourse captivated the audience, but his underlying haughtiness seemed to alienate some, creating a sense of unease in the lecture hall.

Haughtiness means:

a. humility   b. pride   c. meekness

Lachrymose

As the melancholic melody washed over the audience, the renowned pianist poured his emotions into every note, leaving the listeners with a profound sense of sadness. His lachrymose performance resonated deeply, evoking tears and a sense of introspection among those present.

Lachrymose means:

a. tearful   b. joyful   c. happy

Obfuscate

The skilled orator, armed with a plethora of rhetorical devices, effortlessly guided the audience through a maze of intricate arguments and nuanced perspectives. Although his intention was not to confuse, some argued that his clever rhetoric seemed designed to obfuscate the underlying issues and manipulate public opinion.

Obfuscate means:

a. elucidate   b. explain   c. confuse

Plethora

The expansive art gallery showcased a plethora of masterpieces, featuring works from both renowned artists and emerging talents. The vibrant canvases, intricate sculptures, and thought-provoking installations offered a diverse range of artistic expressions, satisfying the aesthetic sensibilities of even the most discerning art enthusiasts.

Plethora means:

a. scarcity   b. dearth   c. profusion

Repudiate

The acclaimed writer, celebrated for her revolutionary ideas and daring narratives, faced backlash for a controversial storyline that challenged societal norms. Undeterred, she chose to stand firm and repudiate the criticism, defending her artistic vision and advocating for the freedom of expression.

Repudiate means:

a. reject   b. embrace   c. endorse

Tedium

Within the hallowed halls of the library, the studious scholar immersed herself in hours of meticulous research and analysis. However, the weight of the extensive readings and the repetitive nature of academic pursuits occasionally led to moments of tedium, prompting her to seek brief respites in the company of friends and engaging in creative hobbies.

Tedium means:

a. monotony   b. excitement   c. interest

Abstemious

In the bustling city, surrounded by an abundance of culinary delights and seductive aromas, the young chef's disciplined approach to food stood out. With a commitment to health and balance, she meticulously curated her menu, showcasing abstemious dishes that delighted the palate without overindulgence, setting a new standard for gastronomic excellence.

Abstemious means:

a. moderate   b. indulgent   c. excessive

Blithe

On a sun-drenched afternoon, a group of carefree friends gathered by the seaside, their laughter filling the air. The blithe spirit of their camaraderie echoed in joyful conversations and playful banter, creating a harmonious atmosphere that transcended the worries of everyday life.

Blithe means:

a. cheerful   b. somber   c. serious

Crepuscular

As the golden hues of dusk painted the sky, an enchanting moment of transition unfolded in the forest. Crepuscular creatures emerged from their daytime hideaways, their silhouettes dancing gracefully in the waning light, as if caught in a whimsical ballet choreographed by nature itself.

Crepuscular means:

a. twilight   b. noonday   c. daytime

Enunciation

In the eloquent embrace of a Shakespearean sonnet, the young actress meticulously crafted each syllable, her enunciation painting vivid pictures in the minds of the captivated audience. Her impeccable delivery, accentuating the beauty of every word, elevated the performance to new heights of artistic mastery.

Enunciation means:

a. mumbling   b. slurring   c. articulation

Headstrong

A determined visionary, the young entrepreneur refused to be swayed by convention or naysayers. With unwavering conviction, she fearlessly pursued her ambitious dreams, charting her own path and proving that being headstrong can be a catalyst for groundbreaking success in a world that often demands conformity.

Headstrong means:

a. stubborn   b. yielding   c. compliant

Lackluster

On the grand stage, the renowned performer, known for her electrifying presence and magnetic charisma, faltered in a lackluster display that left the audience in bewildered disappointment. The absence of her usual spark ignited a profound reflection on the ephemeral nature of artistic brilliance and the vulnerability of even the most celebrated talents.

Lackluster means:

a. dull   b. vibrant   c. exceptional

Objective

The scientist embarked on a rigorous investigation, driven by an unwavering aim to uncover the elusive truth hidden within the depths of the complex phenomenon. With methodical precision, he meticulously designed experiments and tirelessly collected data, leaving no stone upturned in his pursuit of knowledge. Finally, after months of dedication, his objective was achieved, unraveling the mysteries that had confounded his peers.

Objective means:

a. goal   b. subjective   c. biased

Pliable

In the hands of the skilled sculptor, the clay was transformed into a flexible medium, yielding to the artist's touch and assuming intricate shapes and forms. With gentle strokes and careful manipulation, the sculptor molded the pliable material, breathing life into their creative vision. The end result showcased the artist's mastery over this adaptable substance, capturing the fluidity of their artistic expression.

Pliable means:

a. rigid   b. malleable   c. unyielding

Rescind

The oppressive regime had power over the lives of its citizens, dictating their every move and suppressing their basic freedoms. However, the tides of change brought about a glimmer of hope as the people united in their demand to rescind the unjust laws that had plagued their nation for far too long. With relentless determination and unwavering spirit, their collective voice grew louder and stronger, forcing the government to revoke their oppressive policies.

Rescind means:

a. enact
b. repeal
c. instate

Temper

In the midst of a heated argument, emotions flared, threatening to ignite a destructive wildfire. Yet, a wise voice emerged from the chaos, urging everyone to pause, take a deep breath, and alter their responses with rationality and empathy. As each person consciously considered their words, the tension dissipated, replaced by a newfound harmony that stemmed from the collective effort to temper their emotional reactions.

Temper means:

a. agitate
b. moderate
c. escalate

Abstruse

The philosophical discourse rendered the concepts deep, entangling the minds of even the most erudite scholars. Layers upon layers of abstract ideas were woven together, confounding comprehension and challenging the boundaries of human intellect. Yet, amidst the intellectual labyrinth, a select few ventured to decipher the abstruse theories, determined to unlock the profound insights they held.

Abstruse means:

a. complex
b. comprehensible
c. clear

Blunderbuss

In the hands of the inexperienced marksman, the blunderbuss became an instrument of chaos, its lack of precision causing more harm than good. The scattered pellets sprayed in all directions, creating an indiscriminate whirlwind of destruction. However, in the hands of a skilled sharpshooter, it evolved into a powerful weapon, its wide-ranging effect strategically utilized to defeat the most formidable foes.

Blunderbuss means:

a. sniper rifle
b. shotgun
c. precise firearm

Cringe

As the comedian took the stage, the audience eagerly awaited his performance. However, his offensive jokes crossed the line, causing many to cringe in discomfort. The crowd's excitement turned to disappointment as they realized his cringe-inducing humor wasn't what they had anticipated.

Cringe means:

a. applaud   b. flinch   c. admire

Envenom

Within the tight-knit community, a web of gossip began to spread, poisoning relationships and causing distrust among friends. The venomous words uttered by rumor-mongers envenomed minds and hearts, leaving a trail of damaged connections in their wake. It became apparent that the toxic environment needed to be purified through open communication and forgiveness.

Envenom means:

a. heal   b. poison   c. mend

Hedonism

With graduation approaching, Sarah decided to embrace hedonism as a way to celebrate the years of hard work and dedication. She indulged in luxurious spa treatments, delectable cuisine, and thrilling adventures. However, Sarah soon realized that true happiness lay not in hedonism but in finding a balance between pleasure and purpose.

Hedonism means:

a. sensualism   b. asceticism   c. moderation

Laconic

Amidst the bustling classroom, Emily listened attentively while her classmates engaged in lengthy and passionate discussions. When it was her turn to contribute, she conveyed her thoughts concisely and precisely with her laconic style. Despite her few words, Emily's insights carried great depth, leaving her peers in awe.

Laconic means:

a. concise   b. verbose   c. chatty

Oblique

The setting sun cast oblique rays through the dense forest, creating a magical play of light and shadow. As Sarah walked along the path, she noticed an oblique sign pointing towards a hidden trail. Curiosity piqued, she followed the winding path and discovered a breathtaking waterfall nestled amidst the oblique trees.

Laconic means:

a. slanted   b. straight   c. level

Plumage

In the vibrant rainforest, a multitude of birds adorned with colorful plumage darted among the trees. Their feathers glistened in the sunlight, reflecting a dazzling array of hues. Nature enthusiasts marveled at the stunning plumage of these avian creatures, captivated by their beauty and grace.

Plumage means:

a. unfeathered   b. feathers   c. baldness

Resignation

Amelia, a talented violinist, had dedicated countless hours to perfecting her craft. Despite her unwavering commitment, she faced rejection after rejection from prestigious orchestras. With a heavy heart, she ultimately accepted the reality of her situation and made the difficult decision to resign from pursuing a professional music career.

Resignation means:

a. resistance   b. acceptance   c. defiance

Tenacious

David, an aspiring entrepreneur, faced numerous obstacles in launching his business. Despite the setbacks and challenges, he exhibited unwavering determination and a tenacious spirit. Through late nights and countless iterations, he refused to give up, and eventually, his perseverance paid off as his business flourished.

Tenacious means:

a. persistent   b. fickle   c. indecisive

Accolade

Sophia, a brilliant writer, poured her heart and soul into crafting a masterpiece. Her novel garnered critical acclaim and widespread recognition, earning her the highest accolades in the literary world. The prestigious award ceremony celebrated her exceptional talent and marked a defining moment in her career.

Accolade means:

a. honor

b. censure

c. criticism

Bolster

In the face of adversity, Sarah found solace in her closest friends who always provided unwavering support. Their kind words, empathy, and encouragement bolstered her spirits, allowing her to persevere through life's challenges with renewed strength and determination.

Bolster means:

a. weaken

b. deplete

c. fortify

Cryptic

In a dusty attic, Paul stumbled upon an old journal filled with cryptic symbols and enigmatic writings. Intrigued by the mystery, he set out on a quest to decipher the hidden messages and unlock the secrets held within the tattered pages.

Cryptic means:

a. enigmatic

b. explicit

c. transparent

Ephemeral

As the sun dipped below the horizon, casting a radiant display of colors across the sky, Emily couldn't help but admire the ephemeral beauty of the sunset. The fleeting bliss she experienced in that moment served as a poignant reminder to cherish life's transient joys.

Ephemeral means:

a. enduring

b. transient

c. eternal

Acquiesce

In a society governed by rigid hierarchies and unyielding traditions, one must often agree to maintain harmony and avoid discord. This act of surrendering one's own desires and conforming to the collective will requires a profound sense of humility and a willingness to subjugate one's individuality. The ability to acquiesce grants individuals the power to navigate societal complexities with grace and diplomacy.

Acquiesce means:

a. resist   b. comply   c. dissent

Bombast

Within the realm of rhetoric, bombast reigns supreme as an art form that thrives on exaggerated or inflated language. This verbose and grandiloquent style serves as a powerful tool to captivate audiences and sway them to the speaker's perspective. Despite its pomp and flair, it risks diluting the substance of the message and obscuring the speaker's true intentions.

Bombast means:

a. plainness   b. rhetoric   c. conciseness

Curtail

In the pursuit of efficiency and optimization, it often becomes necessary to curtail certain aspects of our lives or endeavors. This deliberate act of reduction ensures that resources are allocated judiciously and goals are achieved with maximum efficacy. Although curtailing may seemingly limit freedom and exploration, it ultimately paves the way for focused growth and the attainment of objectives.

Curtail means:

a. expand   b. encourage   c. restrict

Epicure

One who embraces the title of epicure embarks on a passionate journey of sensory indulgence and refined taste. Armed with discerning palates and an insatiable curiosity, epicures seek to explore the intricacies of cuisine, uncovering the nuances of flavors and textures that ignite the senses. By immersing themselves in this pursuit, they elevate dining experiences to an art form, transcending mere sustenance.

Epicure means:

a. connoisseur   b. ascetic   c. glutton

Heed

In a world brimming with distractions and constant noise, the ability to heed the wisdom embedded within the silence becomes an invaluable skill. Through deliberate contemplation and attentive observation, one can discern the nuanced messages that exist beneath the surface of daily life. By heeding these whispers of truth and intuition, individuals equip themselves with the tools necessary for personal growth and enlightenment.

Heed means:

a. listen   b. overlook   c. ignore

Lampoon

Within comedy, lampoon thrives as a powerful sarcastic tool designed to expose the absurdity and folly of human behavior or societal norms. Through biting humor and exaggerated caricatures, mockery challenges established conventions, prompting introspection and critical analysis. The act of lampooning engenders laughter tinged with incisive social commentary, rendering it a potent force for change and reform.

Lampoon means:

a. satire   b. homage   c. flattery

Hedonist

The hedonist, adorned in luxurious attire and surrounded by opulence, indulged in a life of pleasure and self-gratification. His days were filled with extravagant feasts, lavish parties, and endless pursuits of sensual delights. However, beneath the facade of joy and excess, a deep sense of emptiness lingered, reminding the hedonist that true happiness could not be found in fleeting pleasures alone.

Hedonist means:

a. libertine   b. stoic   c. self-denier

Lamentation

As the mourners gathered, their hearts heavy with grief, a collective lamentation echoed through the air, reverberating with the weight of loss and sorrow. Tears stained their cheeks, and tremors of anguish filled their voices as they expressed their profound grief. The lamentation served as a cathartic release, allowing the mourners to share their pain and find solace in each other's presence.

Lamentation means:

a. elation   b. wailing   c. exultation

Obliterate

Amidst the chaos of war, explosions reverberated through the air, leaving nothing but destruction in their wake. Buildings crumbled, landscapes were charred, and lives were shattered as the relentless onslaught sought to obliterate every trace of normalcy. Yet, within the ruins, a glimmer of hope emerged, reminding the survivors of their resilience and their unwavering spirit to rebuild.

Obliterate means:

a. annihilate   b. preserve   c. restore

Plummet

From great heights, the daredevil acrobat defied gravity, suspended in midair before the crowd's astounded gaze. Then, with a heart-stopping plunge, she relinquished her hold and let gravity take hold. The crowd gasped as they witnessed the acrobat plummet towards the safety net, their faith in the performer's skill creating a tension that dissolved in collective relief as she landed unscathed.

Plummet means:

a. ascend   b. plunge   c. elevate

Resolution

With the chimes of midnight, the new year arrived, accompanied by a surge of resolve. People around the world embraced the opportunity for personal growth, setting lofty goals and crafting detailed plans to bring their aspirations to fruition. Armed with resolute purpose, they faced each obstacle head-on, determined to manifest their dreams and make the upcoming year one of transformation and success.

Resolution means:

a. determination   b. indecisive   c. wavering

Tentative

With timid steps, the novice dancer took his place on the stage, uncertainty flickering in his eyes as he prepared to perform. Tentative movements cautiously wove together, cautiously testing his skill and exploring the boundaries of his technique. Yet, with each passing moment, confidence grew, and his performance blossomed into a captivating display of grace and artistry.

Tentative means:

a. unsure   b. confident   c. resolute

Oblivious

Analyzing self-awareness, one must navigate the delicate balance between perceptive mindfulness and the potential pitfalls of being oblivious. To be oblivious is to exist in a state of blissful ignorance, shielded from both the harsh realities that surround us and the nuanced subtleties that shape our interactions. Often spurred by a desire for self-preservation, individuals choose to remain incognizant to avoid the discomfort and responsibilities that accompany awareness.

Oblivious means:

a. aware   b. ignorant   c. mindful

Podium

The podium stands as an emblem of authority and a beacon of distinction, allowing individuals to command attention and assert their expertise. Standing upon this elevated platform, one confronts both the weight of expectation and the exhilarating potential for influence. Only those who possess the necessary knowledge and charisma can ascend the podium and captivate audiences with their compelling rhetoric.

Podium means:

a. crowd   b. ground   c. platform

Resonant

Deep within the core of human existence lies a yearning for connections that are not only superficial but also deep and resonant. These connections evoke a profound sense of understanding and shared emotions, transcending the boundaries of language and cultural barriers. The resounding echoes of these rolling relationships reverberate through the fabric of our lives, leaving an indelible mark upon our souls.

Resonant means:

a. reverberating   b. flat   c. muted

Tenuous

Like a breakable thread delicately hanging in the balance, weak connections teeter on the precipice of dissolution. These fleeting bonds, often forged through shared experiences or common interests, are easily strained by time, distance, and the complexities of life. While such tenuous connections can be exhilarating in their ephemeral beauty, they also leave individuals vulnerable to the possibility of heartbreak and disconnection.

Tenuous means:

a. string   b. stable   c. fragile

Acrid

From the depths of an industrialized landscape emerges an acrid stench, a reminder of the toll humanity exacts upon the environment. This pungent and noxious odor carries with it the weight of progress and human activities that sacrifice the purity and harmony of nature. As we inhale the acrid air, we awaken to the stark reality of our actions and the urgent need for environmental stewardship.

Acrid means:

a. pungent   b. pleasant   c. aromatic

Boorish

In a society that thrives on civility and cultural refinement, boorish acts stand out as stark reminders of the need for respectful and considerate behavior. Such individual, lacking in manners and social graces, navigates the world with an air of entitlement and disregard for others. By contrast, those who champion empathy and kindness serve as beacons of hope in a landscape often marred by boorishness.

Boorish means:

a. rude   b. polite   c. refined

Cynical

Amidst the rosy hue of youthful optimism, an unpleasant person emerges, armed with skepticism and distrust. This unyielding critic casts a discerning eye upon the world, questioning the authenticity of human motives and the true nature of society. The cynic's perspective, while tinged with a certain bitterness, serves as a reminder to seek the truth beyond the veneer of appearances.

Cynical means:

a. skeptical   b. trusting   c. believing

Epistle

In an era dominated by digital communication, the art of the handwritten epistle has lost its prominence. Yet, within the folds of history, it reigns supreme as a powerful means of expression. Crafted with meticulous care, each stroke of the pen breathes life into the writer's emotions, immortalizing his thoughts within the very fibers of the paper.

Epistle means:

a. verbal   b. missive   c. phone call

Heresy

Heresy lurks as both a threat and an agent of change. It stands in defiance of established doctrines, challenging the very foundations of religious and ideological systems. Though often met with resistance and condemnation, heresy dares to question the status quo, propelling mankind forward on a journey of intellectual growth and spiritual enlightenment.

Heresy means:

a. blasphemy
b. orthodoxy
c. conformity

Lance

From the annals of medieval warfare emerges the formidable and versatile weapon known as the lance. With its gleaming steel tip and sturdy shaft, the lance becomes an extension of the knight's courage and skill. It pierces through the chaos of battle, aiming to unhorse adversaries and assert dominance upon the jousting field.

Lance means:

a. shield
b. retreat
c. spear

Obscure

In the vast sea of knowledge, there exist pockets of obscurity, hidden away from the prying eyes of curiosity. Within these enclaves of the unknown, untapped wisdom and mysteries lie patiently, awaiting the intrepid explorer. To embark upon a quest for knowledge is to unveil the concealed truths and bring them into the realm of understanding.

Obscure means:

a. vague
b. evident
c. well-known

Poignant

As we – humans – have emotions, certain moments leave an indelible mark upon our souls, forever etched in the archives of memory. These poignant encounters evoke a profound sense of empathy, stirring within us a cascade of emotions. They serve as reminders of our shared humanity, transcending borders and fostering connections that unite us in the tapestry of life.

Poignant means:

a. touching
b. trivial
c. unremarkable

Respite

In the relentless flow of life's demands and obligations, the gift of respite emerges like an oasis in the desert. It offers a momentary reprieve, allowing weary souls to rejuvenate and recalibrate. Within the respite's embrace, time slows down, granting solace and liberation from the relentless march of responsibilities.

Respite means:

a. exertion
b. break
c. labor

Terse

In a world inundated with information and noise, brevity reigns as a virtue. The terse language, succinct and to the point, cuts through the cluttered verbosity to convey a potent message. Every word is meticulously chosen, carrying the weight of significance, leaving no room for idle discourse.

Terse means:

a. pithy
b. verbose
c. wordy

Acrophobia

Perched atop a towering precipice, staring into an abyss of vertigo, acrophobia grips its victims with an ironclad fear of heights. The mere sight of vast expanses and dizzying heights sends shivers down the spine, inducing a paralyzing terror. To overcome it requires courage and a determined perseverance to conquer the debilitating phobia.

Acrophobia means:

a. vertigo
b. bravery
c. fearlessness

Bourgeois

Amidst the landscape of societal classes, the bourgeoisie assumes a role, a distinct layer of the upper middle class. The bourgeoisie, vested with wealth and influence, seeks to preserve its privileges and uphold a way of life. Their tastes and values define this specific stratum, while economic disparities and social stratification cast shadows upon their prominence.

Bourgeois means:

a. proletariat
b. middle class
c. working class

Debility

Like an unyielding specter, debility descends upon the body, robbing it of strength and vitality. A formidable adversary, it undermines one's physical and mental faculties, leaving a trail of weakness and incapacitation in its wake. To overcome it demands resilience and unwavering determination to regain lost ground.

Debility means:
a. strength

b. robustness

c. weakness

Epistolary

In literature, the epistolary form serves as a window into the intimate exchanges between characters. Through letters, emotions are bared, secrets unveiled, and connections forged. Epistolary narratives delve into the depths of the human psyche, capturing the raw essence of human experience through the power of the written word.

Epistolary means:
a. verbal

b. written

c. non-literary

Hiatus

In the vast symphony of life, a hiatus presents itself as a fleeting pause, a transient intermission from the relentless rhythm. Within this moment, time elongates, inviting reflection and introspection. It offers an opportunity to recharge, to breathe, before resuming the grand symphony of existence.

Hiatus means:
a. break

b. continuity

c. perpetuity

Languid

Under the weight of exhaustion, the body succumbs to a languid state, moving in slow motion as if submerged in an invisible sea of weariness. Thoughts drift lazily like lapping waves upon a tranquil shore, and limbs seem anchored by an invisible force. Yet within these special moments, the mind finds solace and respite.

Languid means:
a. dynamic

b. lethargic

c. animated

Obscured

A thick fog descends upon the landscape, enveloping the world in a shroud of uncertainty. Vision becomes blurred, contours are lost, and familiarity fades away. Objects once discernible now appear as mere silhouettes, concealed beneath the veil of obscurity. Yet even amid such ambiguity, clarity will eventually pierce through, dispelling the obscured.

Obscured means:

a. revealed　　　　b. clouded　　　　c. obvious

Poised

With quiet confidence and unwavering grace, she stands poised on the precipice of possibility, ready to embrace the unknown. Like a dancer frozen in mid-air, every muscle and thought aligns, awaiting the perfect moment to unfurl. Self-contend, she takes the leap, defying gravity and etching her own path.

Poised means:

a. unsteady　　　　b. clumsy　　　　c. confident

Resplendent

As the sun reaches its zenith, casting a radiant glow upon the earth, the world awakens to a resplendent display of colors and light. Nature's palette unfolds, painting the sky with hues of gold, crimson, and sapphire. Within this splendid tapestry, beauty and harmony intertwine, captivating all who behold it.

Resplendent means:

a. dazzling　　　　b. dull　　　　c. drab

Therapeutic

A healthful connection between mind, body, and spirit emerges, fostering a pathway towards wholeness. Through art, movement, or conversation, wounds begin to mend, burdens ease, and transformation unfolds. Therapeutic spaces become sanctuaries, providing solace and a flickering light of hope.

Therapeutic means:

a. curative　　　　b. detrimental　　　　c. harmful

Acuity

With remarkable acuity, her senses absorbed every detail of the world around her. The delicate whispers of the wind, the subtle play of light and shadow, and the symphony of scents that danced upon the air. Through her perceptive gaze, the intricacies of life unfolded, revealing a tapestry of wonders that epitomized the richness of existence.

Acuity means:

a. sharpness   b. obtuseness   c. obliviousness

Braggart

With an inflated ego and an insatiable need for validation, the braggart sought to proclaim his perceived greatness to all who would listen. He boasted of achievements both real and imagined, weaving tales of grandeur within his self-centered narrative. But beneath the facade of arrogance lay a fragile self-esteem that would ultimately languish in the face of truth.

Braggart means:

a. egotist   b. modest   c. unassuming

Debunking

Armed with reason and a dedication to authentic knowledge, the debunkers dismantled the webs of falsehoods that ensnared the minds of the misinformed. Diligently examining claims, scrutinizing evidence, and unraveling fallacies, they exposed the truth that lay concealed beneath layers of deception. Through meticulous analysis, the debunks resolved to confront ignorance with unwavering clarity.

Debunking means:

a. refute   b. confirm   c. validate

Epitomized

In the figure of the noble knight, honor, chivalry, and integrity converged with unwavering purpose. Through courageous acts and selfless deeds, he epitomized the embodiment of virtue. His shining armor glistened in the sun as a symbol of strength and righteousness, his very essence reflecting an ideal that inspired others to aspire to greatness.

Epitomized means:

a. defy   b. betray   c. embody

Hidebound

Bound by tradition and resistant to change, the hidebound society clung tightly to its established norms and customs. Innovations were met with skepticism, and alternative perspectives were dismissed as heresy. In the face of progress, this strict adherence to the past limited growth and stifled creativity, relegating the community to languish in a stagnant state.

Hidebound means:
a. flexible   b. adaptable   c. rigid

Languish

Locked within the confines of despair, a soul began to languish, losing the essence of vitality that once thrived within. Hope withered like a fragile flower starved of sunlight, suffocating under the weight of desolation. Yet amidst the darkness, a flicker of resilience emerged, a whisper of strength that yearned to break free and banish the shadows.

Languish means:
a. thrive   b. prosper   c. wither

Obsequious

In the court of the imperious king, the obsequious courtier bowed low, his gestures steeped in exaggerated subservience. Every word spoken was laced with honeyed flattery, an artful display of sycophantic charm. His servile nature sought to appease, yet beneath the facade of unwavering loyalty, his true intentions remained shrouded.

Obsequious means:
a. servile   b. assertive   c. defiant

Polemical

Engaged in a fervent debate, the intellectual titans clashed, wielding words as their mighty weapons. Each thrust and parry was executed with eloquence and precision, as they sought to dismantle their opponent's arguments. Passion fueled their rhetoric, igniting a polemical battlefield where reason and persuasion battled for supremacy.

Polemical means:
a. controversial   b. conciliatory   c. diplomatic

Restorative

Amidst the chaos and turmoil, the weary traveler found solace in the embrace of nature's restorative beauty. The tranquil meadows whispered with serenity, and the gentle caress of the breeze brought vigor to their fatigued soul. In this sanctuary of peace, the harmony of existence blossomed, offering a respite from the weariness of the world.

Restorative means:

a. rejuvenating
b. draining
c. enervating

Thwart

With cunning strategy and unwavering determination, the protagonists sought to thwart the villain's nefarious plot. They navigated treacherous obstacles, evaded countless traps, and outwitted their adversary at every turn. In the climactic battle, their resilience prevailed, and the imminent catastrophe was narrowly averted.

Thwart means:

a. hinder
b. assist
c. facilitate

Adamant

Unyielding in her convictions, she stood adamant in the face of adversity. No amount of persuasion or coercion could sway her resolve. With unwavering determination, she pursued her chosen path, impervious to the doubts and criticisms that sought to undermine her. Her steadfastness became a beacon of strength in a world of wavering opinions.

Adamant means:

a. resolute
b. indecisive
c. wavering

Brawny

Covered in glistening sweat, the brawny laborer showcased the fruits of his physical toil. Every muscle rippled with strength and power as he effortlessly lifted heavy burdens and conquered arduous tasks. His physique, sculpted through relentless work, epitomized the embodiment of physical prowess.

Brawny means:

a. weak
b. muscular
c. delicate

Decathlon

With unwavering dedication and relentless training, the aspiring athlete prepared for the ultimate test of versatility and endurance - the decathlon. Ten grueling events awaited, each demanding a different set of physical and mental skills. From sprinting to shot-put, pole vault to long jump, the decathlete's prowess in each discipline would be on full display, culminating in a triumphant showcase of their athletic prowess.

Decathlon means:

a. multisport competition   b. single event   c. focused training

Equivocate

In politics, where words are chosen with calculated precision, the art of evasion thrives. With cleverly crafted rhetoric and strategic ambiguity, politicians navigate treacherous terrain, skillfully avoiding commitment and maintaining plausible deniability. Their mastery of equivocation leaves room for interpretation, allowing them to skirt controversy and appeal to diverse audiences.

Equivocate means:

a. specify   b. hedge   c. affirm

Hieroglyphics

Etched upon the ancient walls of tombs and temples, they tell stories of long-forgotten civilizations. These intricate symbols, a visual tapestry of meaning, are a portal into the mysteries of the past. Scholars tirelessly decipher these cryptic codes, unlocking the secrets hidden within the enigmatic world of hieroglyphics.

Hieroglyphics means:

a. plain text   b. symbols   c. modern writing

Larceny

During the night, the stealthy thieves surreptitiously infiltrated the opulent mansion, driven by a hunger for ill-gotten wealth. With nimble fingers and a devious mind, they navigated the maze-like corridors, greedily snatching valuable artifacts and precious jewels. Yet, the price of their larceny would eventually catch up with them, for no riches acquired through dishonorable means could bring true fulfillment.

Larceny means:

a. honesty   b. theft   c. integrity

Obsession

Consumed by an all-consuming obsession, the artist poured his heart, soul, and every waking minute into his craft. His mind became a swirling vortex of ideas and possibilities, an insatiable hunger for perfection. To create, to express, to bring his vision to life was an indomitable force that propelled him forward.

Obsession means:

a. fixation   b. apathy   c. disinterest

Ponderous

The ancient tome, adorned with faded leather and worn pages, was a ponderous weight in the hands of the eager scholar. Line after line of intricate prose revealed a labyrinthine depth of knowledge, requiring careful contemplation and intellectual acuity to navigate. Each word held the potential to unlock profound insights, beckoning the reader into a world of boundless discovery.

Ponderous means:

a. light   b. agile   c. weighty

Retention

Within education, the concept of retention occupies a prominent role. It refers to the ability of students to remember and apply the knowledge they have acquired. The efficacy of teaching methods and the depth of understanding can be measured by the degree of retentivity exhibited by students. With retention as the ultimate goal, educators employ various strategies to enhance learning and ensure lasting comprehension.

Retention means:

a. amnesia   b. loss   c. memory

Timorous

In the face of adversity, the timorous individual quivers with trepidation, their confidence waning like a flickering candle in the wind. Fear and anxiousness plague his every step, leaving him paralyzed by doubt and uncertainty. Only with courage and resilience can the trepid break free from their self-imposed shackles and embrace the boundless possibilities that await.

Timorous means:

a. bold   b. timid   c. audacious

Adroit

With an adroit hand, the accomplished artisan manipulates the delicate threads of fabric, turning mere textile into a masterpiece. His nimble fingers deftly navigate the loom, weaving intricate patterns and blending colors harmoniously. It is through his adroit craftsmanship that the essence of artistry is brought to life.

Adroit means:

a. clumsy

b. skillful

c. inept

Brevity

In communication, brevity is a virtue heightened by the scarcity of time and attention. Succinct and concise, this art demands clarity and precision in conveying ideas efficiently. It is through brevity that words acquire power, delivering a potent impact with minimal expenditure.

Brevity means:

a. conciseness

b. verbosity

c. prolixity

Decorum

Within the hallowed halls of diplomacy, decorum reigns supreme. It is an unwritten code of conduct, dictating the proper behavior and etiquette expected from individuals in formal settings. Adhering to it ensures a harmonious and respectful atmosphere, where divergent perspectives are discussed with civility and decorous grace.

Decorum means:

a. rudeness

b. disrespect

c. propriety

Err

In the intricate dance of life, even the most astute minds are not immune to occasional missteps. To err is to acknowledge the inherent fallibility of human nature, to recognize that mistakes are opportune moments for growth and learning. It is through the process of erring and self-correction that individuals pave their path towards wisdom and enlightenment.

Err means:

a. blunder

b. acumen

c. infallibility

Hinder

Progress in any endeavor can be hindered by various factors, impeding the forward momentum and obstructing the path to success. Unforeseen obstacles and challenges often arise, posing significant barriers that demand resilience and resourcefulness to overcome. It is the ability to confront and surmount these hindrances that separates the ordinary from the extraordinary.

Hinder means:

a. impede

b. assist

c. facilitate

Largess

In the annals of history, the noble act of bestowing largess upon the less fortunate has long been revered. Generosity in abundance, this act transcends simple charity, embodying a profound empathy for the plight of others. Its true essence lies not in the material wealth shared, but in the immeasurable impact it has on the recipients' lives.

Largess means:

a. generosity

b. stinginess

c. greed

Obsolete

Time's relentless march renders many technologies and once-vital systems obsolete, relics of a bygone era. The rapid pace of innovation and the unyielding demands of progress consign older models to irrelevance. However, amidst the ever-changing landscape, one must remember that obsolescence is not merely an end, but a catalyst for new beginnings.

Obsolete means:

a. current

b. outdated

c. contemporary

Pontificate

The renowned sage, draped in robes of wisdom, ascends the pulpit to pontificate on matters of great import. His eloquent words resonate, offering guidance and insight to those who seek enlightenment. Yet, amidst the grandeur of his rhetoric, one must remember that true wisdom lies not solely in pontification, but in the humble application of knowledge.

Pontificate means:

a. lecture

b. listen

c. learn

Reticent

Behind a curtain of reticence, the introverted souls hides, their thoughts and emotions concealed from prying eyes. They prefer the solace of introspection and observe from the periphery, seldom revealing their innermost truths. But let us remember, reticence should be met with understanding, as silence often carries wisdom that words fail to capture.

Reticent means:

a. talkative   b. extroverted   c. reserved

Tirade

As the tempestuous storm rages within, a torrent of passionate words pours forth in a fierce tirade. The speaker's voice booms, his anger and frustration unleashed with each tumultuous sentence. Yet, beneath the surface of this verbal outburst, lies a plea for understanding, a desperate attempt to be heard amidst the chaos.

Tirade means:

a. praise   b. adulation   c. diatribe

Adulation

Through fame and fortune, adulation often follows in the wake of extraordinary achievements. The applause and adoration bestowed upon those who reach the pinnacle of success can be intoxicating, fueling passion further. However, amidst the sea of adoration, one must remain grounded, for true fulfillment lies not in the flattery itself, but in the pursuit of one's dreams.

Adulation means:

a. worship   b. disdain   c. scorn

Bristle

In the face of adversity, a person's character may bristle, revealing a fierce determination and resilience. Like the spines of a porcupine standing on end, his unwavering resolve can serve as a shield against the challenges that threaten to overwhelm. It is in these moments that true strength emerges, sharp and unyielding.

Bristle means:

a. sooth   b. uncurl   c. bridle

Decoy

In the intricate game of strategy, a decoy is an invaluable tool, diverting attention and luring opponents into a carefully woven trap. Like a skilled puppeteer pulling the strings, the mastermind manipulates the pieces on the board, enticing their adversaries into making fatal mistakes. A well-executed decoy can turn the tide of battle, leaving their unsuspecting opponent bewildered in its wake.

Decoy means:

a. lure   b. genuine   c. authentic

Erratic

Life's journey is often marked by unpredictable twists and turns, a winding path that leads us through moments of both triumph and tribulation. The erratic nature of existence keeps us on our toes, challenging us to adapt and embrace the unknown. Amidst the chaos, we must find solace in knowing that every erratic step holds the potential for growth and self-discovery.

Erratic means:

a. stable   b. volatile   c. steady

Histrionic

The stage becomes a canvas upon which emotions are painted, each performer wielding their histrionic abilities to captivate the audience. Their exaggerated gestures and striking expressions bring the characters to life, evoking laughter, tears, and empathy. Yet, beyond the dazzling theatrics, lies a profound exploration of the human condition, a mirror held up to society's joys and sorrows.

Histrionic means:

a. dramatic   b. subdued   c. understated

Laud

To laud someone's achievements is to celebrate triumphs with resounding applause, acknowledging hard work and dedication. The reverberating echoes of praise resound through the corridors of success, uplifting the spirits of the deserving. In the act of lauding another, we not only honor accomplishments but also inspire others to strive for greatness.

Laud means:

a. acclaim   b. condemn   c. disparage

Obstreperous

In the tranquil classroom, where silence and order reigned supreme, there was one student who consistently disrupted the delicate balance. With an unyielding spirit and a boisterous nature, he embraced his role as the class clown, injecting moments of chaos into the teacher's meticulously planned lessons. Despite his obstreperous behavior, his mischievous antics occasionally revealed an underlying brilliance, providing glimpses of untapped potential.

Obstreperous means:

a. quiet   b. unruly   c. docile

Portend

As the dark clouds gathered ominously on the horizon, a sense of foreboding enveloped the townsfolk. Nature's subtle signposts seemed to portend impending doom, their whispers in the wind echoing tales of impending tempests and catastrophic events. With bated breath, they awaited the revelation of what fate had in store for their once peaceful village.

Portend means:

a. assure   b. predict   c. indicate

Retraction

In the cutthroat world of journalism, the power of words cannot be underestimated. However, even the most skilled writer occasionally stumbles, unintentionally penning falsehoods that stain their reputation. It is in these moments of vulnerability that the art of the retraction flourishes, with each carefully chosen word serving as a balm to mend the wounds inflicted upon veracity.

Retraction means:

a. withdrawal   b. claim   c. assertion

Titter

In the opulent ballroom, hushed whispers and stifled laughter filled the air as the guests exchanged glances during an awkward exchange. A titter, delicate yet contagious, escaped from the lips of a young debutante, like a fizzing champagne bubble bursting free. The subtle amusement danced across their refined expressions, bridging the divide between formality and fleeting mirth.

Titter means:

a. giggle   b. guffaw   c. roar

Adversity

Life's journey is paved with hurdles and obstacles, challenging our resilience and testing our mettle. Adversity, like a formidable opponent, emerges unexpectedly, threatening to derail our ambitions and dreams. Yet, it is within the crucible of struggle that our true character is forged, as we tenaciously rise above the adversities that seek to break our spirit.

Adversity means:

a. hardship   b. success   c. ease

Broach

Amidst delicate conversations, there are certain matters that require finesse when broaching the subject. With careful consideration, one must navigate the treacherous waters of diplomacy, delicately opening the door to taboo topics. The art lies in finding the balance between honesty and sensitivity, ensuring that the outcome is conducive to understanding and growth.

Broach means:

a. introduce   b. avoid   c. evade

Deference

In the grand halls of the palace, a culture of deference prevailed, transforming the interactions between the subjects and their regal sovereign. Each bow and curtsy was an homage to the power and wisdom embodied by their ruler, an act of humble recognition of the vast responsibilities shouldered by the throne. The deference was palpable in their collective spirit, a testament to the enduring tradition of respect.

Deference means:

a. respect   b. insolence   c. defiance

Esoteric

Inside the hallowed halls of academia, there exists a realm of knowledge that transcends the boundaries of common understanding. The esoteric subjects and theories discussed among scholars are like ancient ciphered texts, decipherable only by those who possess the key to the intellectual labyrinth. Hidden beneath intricately layered concepts, knowledge waits to be unraveled by those with an insatiable thirst for enlightenment.

Esoteric means:

a. arcane   b. common   c. mundane

Hoary

In the chilling embrace of winter, the landscape underwent a remarkable transformation as a blanket of hoary frost settled upon the earth. Each delicate branch, laden with icicles, appeared as if touched by the hand of an artist, glistening in the soft sunlight. The hoary scenes created a timeless beauty, as if nature had frozen a moment in history.

Hoary means:

a. new   b. vibrant   c. frosty

Lavish

In the opulent ballroom, the guests reveled in an atmosphere of extravagance, surrounded by lavish decorations and shimmering chandeliers. The tables were adorned with elaborate floral arrangements, and servers presented platters of succulent delicacies fit for royalty. Every detail of the event exuded a luxury that left a lasting impression on the attendees.

Lavish means:

a. extravagant   b. modest   c. frugal

Obtuse

Despite the professor's best efforts to simplify the complex concepts, one student remained perpetually befuddled, staring blankly as obtuse ideas floated past, just beyond their grasp. The frustration of their peers grew as the student's obtuseness hindered the progress of the class, leaving the professor struggling to bridge the divide between comprehension and confusion.

Obtuse means:

a. astute   b. sharp   c. dull

Portent

In the eerie stillness of the night, an air of anticipation settled over the town, sensing a portent of events yet to unfold. It was as if the cosmos conspired to send a message through the alignment of stars and the whispers of the wind. The sign hung heavy in the atmosphere, leaving the inhabitants on edge, awaiting the revelation of what fate had in store for them.

Portent means:

a. omen   b. normalcy   c. dismissal

Revere

In the heart of the ancient temple, devotees congregated to pay homage to their revered deity, displaying unwavering loyalty and veneration. The essence of their faith was palpable, as they approached the altar with a reverence that transcended the realm of mortal comprehension. The worshippers found solace in the belief that their reverential acts bridged the gap between the mortal and the divine.

Revere means:

a. idolize   b. scorn   c. despise

Tome

Adorned with weathered leather and aged pages, the heavy tome rested upon the shelf, emitting an aura of knowledge amassed through the centuries. Its words, etched by scholars long past, offered a glimpse into worlds unknown, inviting readers into a realm of infinite possibilities. As the reader delved into the intricate tales and profound insights held within the tome's ancient bindings, they embraced the power of literature to transport and enlighten.

Tome means:

a. volume   b. pamphlet   c. leaflet

Advocate

With unwavering conviction, the passionate advocate took the stand, his voice resounding with clarity and purpose. His arguments cascaded with eloquence, appealing to reason and evoking an undeniable sense of justice. His unwavering dedication to their cause transcended personal gain, embodying the spirit of those who championed for a more equitable society.

Advocate means:

a. opponent   b. critic   c. supporter

Brusque

The brusque delivery of the professor's remarks left the students startled, caught off guard by the sharpness of the words. With a laconic tone and dismissive gestures, the professor seemed to have little regard for the sensitivity of his audience. His brusqueness hindered the learning process, undermining the open exchange of ideas that should have been fostered within the academic community.

Brusque means:

a. polite   b. curt   c. tactful

Defoliate

As autumn's arrival announced the changing of seasons, the once lush forest transformed into a canvas of vibrant hues before surrendering to winter's impending arrival. The leaves danced in a graceful descent, a mesmerizing spectacle as they gradually defoliated the trees. With every gentle breeze, the forest embraced its metamorphosis, preparing for renewal and the promise of growth in the seasons to come.

Defoliate means:

a. strip   b. clothe   c. adorn

Espouse

The philosopher expounded upon her revolutionary ideas, fervently espousing a new way of thinking that challenged the prevailing wisdom. She sought to inspire the masses, encouraging them to embrace the principles that would lead to societal transformation. The philosopher's desire to espouse these principles stemmed from a genuine yearning to create a more enlightened and inclusive world.

Espouse means:

a. support   b. reject   c. oppose

Hone

With unwavering determination, the aspiring chef meticulously crafted each dish, delicately adjusting the flavors to achieve perfection. The hours spent in the bustling kitchen were dedicated to honing his culinary skills, sharpening his ability to transform ordinary ingredients into culinary masterpieces. Through trial and error, the chef's relentless pursuit of excellence allowed him to refine his culinary techniques and elevate his creations to unparalleled heights.

Hone means:

a. refine   b. worsen   c. blunt

Lax

In the face of mounting deadlines and pressing responsibilities, the students once unwavering discipline began to wane, replaced by a lax approach to their academic obligations. Time once spent studying and preparing for examinations was now squandered on distractions, leading to a decline in performance. As the consequences of their attitude became apparent, the students realized the need to regain focus and recommit to their educational journey.

Lax means:

a. stringent   b. lenient   c. vigilant

Obviate

The innovative invention presented a groundbreaking solution, effectively obviating the need for labor-intensive manual tasks. Through the integration of cutting-edge technology, the inefficiencies that plagued traditional practices were eradicated. The newfound efficiency ushered in a wave of progress, streamlining operations and propelling industries towards unprecedented growth.

Obviate means:

a. eliminate   b. require   c. mandate

Poseur

In the bohemian art gallery, a figure stood amidst the vibrant canvases, radiating an air of pretentiousness and insincerity. The poseur's carefully curated persona, clad in eccentric attire and adorned with ostentatious accessories, aimed to deceive others into believing they possessed a profound artistic sensibility. Yet, beneath the façade, an emptiness riddled their existence, a yearning for genuine self-expression that eluded their superficial endeavors.

Poseur means:

a. authentic   b. humble   c. pretender

Riddled

As the detective meticulously examined the crime scene, a myriad of clues beckoned their attention, each tantalizingly pointing towards the truth. The evidence, riddled with enigmatic symbols and cryptic messages, seemed intent on challenging the detective's intellect and deductive reasoning. With every puzzle solved and every mystery unraveled, the detective inched closer to capturing the elusive culprit.

Riddled means:

a. filled   b. clear   c. devoid

Torpid

Within the expanse of the frozen tundra, a polar bear lay in a state of torpor, conserving its energy during the harsh winter months. The bear's metabolism slowed to a crawl, rendering it in a dormant state, waiting for the arrival of more favorable conditions. As spring emerged, the bear emerged from its torpid slumber, renewed and ready to resume the cycle of life in the unforgiving Arctic landscape.

Torpid means:

a. lively   b. dormant   c. vibrant

Aesthetic

The art gallery showcased a captivating collection of paintings, carefully curated to evoke a sense of beauty and harmony. Each brushstroke and color palette was thoughtfully selected to create an aesthetic experience that transcended the boundaries of ordinary perception. As visitors wandered through the gallery, they stood in awe of the artistry displayed before them, their senses captivated by the symphony of visual allure.

Aesthetic means:

a. ugly   b. bland   a. artistic

Bulwark

In times of uncertainty and turmoil, a unified community stands as a barrier against the storms that threaten to engulf society. Bound by shared values and a sense of purpose, individuals join forces to protect the cherished ideals on which their civilization is built. Through collective action and unwavering resilience, they form an impenetrable bulwark against the forces that seek to sow discord and division.

Bulwark means:

a. fortress   b. gap   c. vulnerability

Defunct

Once a bustling hub of activity, the abandoned factory now stood as a haunting reminder of a bygone era. The machinery, once a testament to industrial innovation, now lay dormant and obsolete, no longer capable of fulfilling its intended purpose. The defunct factory, shrouded in silence, served as a poignant symbol of the passage of time and the inevitable evolution of progress.

Defunct means:

a. inactive   b. operational   c. live

Etymology

Language enthusiasts delved deep into the root and etymology of words, unearthing the rich tapestry of their linguistic heritage. Its study allowed them to trace the evolution of language, unravelling the intricate webs of connections between words and their historical roots. By unraveling the etymology of words, they gained profound insights into the cultural and linguistic heritage of humanity.

Etymology means:

a. current usage   b. word origin   c. current meaning

Hyperbole

With each exaggerated gesture and embellished phrase, the storyteller transported its audience into realms of imagination and wonder. Hyperbole, a literary tool employed for dramatic effect, lent an air of grandiosity to their tales. The audience hung on every word, delighting in the writer's skillful use of hyperbole to elevate the mundane into the extraordinary, and the ordinary into the realm of legend.

Hyperbole means:

a. understatement   b. exaggeration   c. accuracy

Legend

Across generations, stories were passed down, weaving together to form the tapestry of folklore and myth. Legends, steeped in mysticism and imagination, offered glimpses into the past and spoke of heroic deeds and larger-than-life figures. Through these narratives, societies preserved their collective memory and celebrated the extraordinary feats that had shaped their culture and identity.

Legend means:

a. myth   b. fact   c. reality

Odious

In the dimly lit cellar, a pungent and repulsive odor filled the air, rendering it almost unbearable. The source of this odious stench was an ancient, decaying pile of garbage that had been left unattended for far too long. The mere thought of its putrid contents sent shivers down one's spine, reminding them of the unsettling nature of all things foul.

Odious means:

a. repugnant   b. pleasant   c. agreeable

Posterity

The great leaders of the past, driven by a sense of duty and vision, tirelessly toiled to create a better world for posterity. They crafted policies and built institutions, always mindful of the lasting impact their actions would have on future generations. Their efforts were not in vain, for their wisdom and foresight continue to shape the destiny of men.

Posterity means:

a. ancestors   b. descendants   c. forebears

Rife

In the midst of political unrest, rumors and conspiracy theories ran rife throughout the nation. Misinformation spread like wildfire, casting a shadow of doubt and apprehension over the populace. The power of social media platforms amplified these false narratives, leaving people disillusioned and uncertain about the veracity of the information presented to them.

Rife means:

a. prevalent   b. scarce   c. limited

Torpor

Under the scorching sun, the lizard basked lazily on a sun-kissed rock, its movements slow and dazed. The heat of the day had enveloped the reptile, inducing a state of torpor that allowed it to conserve energy and endure the harsh conditions of its arid habitat. With each passing minute, the lizard's passivity persisted, masking its inherent alertness.

Torpor means:

a. energy   b. liveliness   c. lethargy

Affable

With a warm smile and kind words, the host welcomed each guest into their home, creating an atmosphere of conviviality and genuine friendship. Their affable nature put everyone at ease, encouraging lively conversations and fostering a sense of camaraderie. Long after the evening had ended, the memory of his hospitality lingered in the hearts of those fortunate enough to have attended.

Affable means:

a. aloof   b. hostile   c. amiable

Bureaucracy

Navigating the intricate labyrinth of bureaucracy proved to be a daunting task, as paperwork piled up and forms multiplied. Countless hours were spent on hold, waiting for an elusive government official to address one's concerns. The red tape and rigid procedures seemed interminable, creating a sense of frustration and impeding progress at every turn.

Bureaucracy means:

a. administration   b. efficiency   c. directness

Degradation

The once magnificent mansion stood in a state of decrepitude, a stark contrast to its former glory. Time had ravaged its grand facade, leaving behind crumbling walls and sagging floors. The degradation of this architectural gem was a poignant reminder of the inherent transience of all things.

Degradation means:

a. improvement
b. restoration
c. decay

Eulogy

The room fell into a hushed silence as the speaker approached the podium to deliver a heartfelt eulogy. With eloquence and grace, he recounted the remarkable life of the revered individual who had left an indelible mark on the hearts of many. This served as a testament to his profound impact even after death.

Eulogy means:

a. tribute
b. denunciation
c. criticism

Hypochondriac

Every slight ache or minor malaise sent the hypochondriac into a state of panic, convinced he was suffering from a grave illness. His mind was plagued by imagined symptoms and exaggerated fears, causing unnecessary distress. The hypochondriac's preoccupation with health became an all-consuming obsession.

Hypochondriac means:

a. stoic
b. nonchalant
c. worrier

Legion

An army of thousands, clad in formidable armor and marching with unwavering discipline, descended upon the battlefield. This formidable legion of warriors instilled fear in the hearts of their adversaries. With unwavering resolve, they fought valiantly, unyielding in their mission to protect their homeland.

Legion means:

a. handful
b. multitude
c. individual

Officious

The officious clerk behind the counter scrutinized every detail of the paperwork, determined to enforce the rules to the letter. His over-zealousness created unnecessary obstacles and delays, frustrating those seeking assistance. The officious behavior dampened the atmosphere, leaving visitors feeling unwelcome and disheartened.

Officious means:

a. easygoing   b. intrusive   c. laid-back

Posthumous

The artist's final masterpiece was unveiled to the world after his untimely demise, marking the beginning of his posthumous recognition. The brilliance and innovation displayed in this last work solidified his place among the legends of the art world. The artist's creative legacy lived on, even after their physical presence had faded away.

Posthumous means:

a. antemortem   b. postmortem   c. during life

Rigor

In the pursuit of scientific knowledge, researchers subject their theories and hypotheses to tight scrutiny and experimentation. The systematic application of logical reasoning and empirical evidence ensures that their conclusions are sound and reliable. Through the rigorous scientific process, new discoveries are made, and existing knowledge is expanded.

Rigor means:

a. strictness   b. leniency   c. laxity

Totter

With each unsteady step, the frail old woman tottered along the narrow cobblestone path, leaning on her trusted cane for support. Age had rendered her body weak and unstable, her once nimble gait reduced to a cautious shuffle. Despite her tottering presence, her spirit remained resilient and determined.

Totter means:

a. teeter   b. stride   c. strut

Alchemy

In alchemy, an ancient art of transforming base metals into precious substances, practitioners sought to unlock the secrets of the universe. The alchemist's laboratory was filled with mysterious potions and bubbling beakers, as he diligently pursued the elusive elixir of life. His ultimate ambition was to achieve the alchemical transformation of lead into gold.

Alchemy means:

a. sorcery   b. science   c. materialism

Burnish

With skilled hands, the artisan meticulously polished the surface of the silver teapot, eager to bring out its natural luster. The careful application of gentle strokes and polishing compounds ensured that every imperfection was eradicated and the teapot gleamed with a burnished brilliance. The meticulous burnishing process transformed the teapot into a work of art.

Burnish means:

a. tarnish   b. corrode   c. shine

Deliberate

The jury members gathered in the deliberation room, ready to carefully consider the evidence presented during the trial. Each juror took its responsibility seriously, engaging in thoughtful dialogue and analysis. After hours of deliberate discussion, they reached a unanimous verdict: guilty.

Deliberate means:

a. hasty   b. thoughtful   c. impulsive

Euphony

As the orchestra struck their first chords, a melodious symphony filled the auditorium, enveloping the audience in a soothing sea of auditory sensation. The harmonious blend of instruments created aural poetry that transcended the boundaries of language. The enchanting euphony of the orchestra captivated the listeners, transporting them to another realm.

Euphony means:

a. cacophony   b. melody   c. noise

Iconoclast

Throughout history, society has often revered established norms and deeply held beliefs. However, every now and then, an iconoclast emerges, challenging the status quo and questioning the very foundations upon which society stands. These fearless individuals fear no reprisal as they smash the idols of tradition, paving the way for new ideas and perspectives.

Iconoclast means:

a. rebel   b. conformist   c. follower

Levity

Amid a somber gathering, one person's lighthearted remarks served as a ray of sunshine, momentarily lifting the heaviness from the room. The subtle frivolity injected a much-needed sense of humor, reminding everyone that laughter has the power to heal and unite. Their witty banter and playful gestures created an atmosphere of joy and levity.

Levity means:

a. buoyancy   b. solemnity   c. seriousness

Olfactory

As the scent of freshly brewed coffee and warm croissants wafted through the air, the olfactory senses of the patrons awakened, tantalizing their nostrils with a sense of anticipation. The rich, earthy notes mingled with the sweet hints of vanilla, creating a sensory symphony that elevated the dining experience to a whole new level.

Olfactory means:

a. odorless   b. aroma   c. odoriferous

Potable

In arid regions where water is scarce, the discovery of a natural spring with potable water is cause for celebration. The crystal-clear liquid, free from contaminants and impurities, sustains life and quenches the thirst of both humans and wildlife alike, ensuring their survival in harsh climates.

Potable means:

a. drinkable   b. impure   c. undrinkable

Rotund

The distinguished gentleman, with his round belly straining against the buttons of his tailored suit, exuded an air of affluence and indulgence. His rotund figure bore witness to a life well-lived, where culinary delights and lavish feasts were the norm. Yet, beneath his ample girth, lay a compassionate heart and a sharp intellect that inspired respect from all who encountered him.

Rotund means:

a. lean   b. slender   c. plump

Tranquil

Nestled amidst a verdant landscape, a small cottage stood in perfect harmony with its surroundings. The tranquility of the sprawling gardens and the gentle ripple of a nearby brook created a haven of serenity. In this idyllic retreat, one could experience true solace and peace, far removed from the chaos and tumult of the outside world.

Tranquil means:

a. serene   b. chaotic   c. tumultuous

Alibi

In the dimly lit room, the accused sat composed, ready to present his alibi to the jurors who would ultimately determine his fate. With unwavering confidence, he recounted the events of that fateful night, meticulously constructing a plausible narrative that would cast doubt upon his involvement in the crime. His carefully crafted story, aimed to establish an airtight defense against the charges he faced.

Alibi means:

a. excuse   b. prosecution   c. guilt

Buttress

Standing tall against the test of time, the ancient castle showcased its formidable grandeur with a series of monumental buttresses that fortified its walls. These solid structures, intricately designed and expertly engineered, served as architectural supports, ensuring the stability and longevity of the castle's towering edifice. Their purpose was to reinforce the structural integrity, shielding the castle from external forces.

Buttress means:

a. weaken   b. support   c. dismantle

Delineation

Amidst the world of art, the skillful artist employed precise brushstrokes to bring life to its subjects, capturing intricate details with meticulous delineation. Every line, every stroke mattered, illustrating not just the physical attributes but also the essence and character of each subject. Through the artist's masterful delineation, a vivid and authentic portrayal was achieved.

Delineation means:

a. depiction   b vagueness   c. ambiguity

Evacuate

With the rising floodwaters, panic and chaos ensued as residents in low-lying areas scrambled to evacuate, seeking higher ground and safety. The urgency in the air was palpable as families hurriedly packed their belongings, desperate to escape the imminent disaster. Through organized efforts and swift action, authorities successfully facilitated the smooth evacuation of the affected areas.

Evacuate means:

a. vacate   b. occupy   c. inhabit

Idiosyncrasy

In a world where conformism often reigns supreme, the eccentric professor embraced his mannerism with pride and defiance. With his unruly hair, mismatched socks, and unconventional teaching methods, he became a beloved figure among his students. His idiosyncrasies were not perceived as flaws but rather as unique traits that set him apart and added color to his persona.

Idiosyncrasy means:

a. normality   b. peculiarity   c. conformity

Libertarian

Rooted in the principles of individual freedom and limited government intervention, the movement attracted those who sought to maximize personal liberty and minimize external constraints. Advocates of this ideology championed free markets, limited taxation, and individual autonomy as the cornerstones of a prosperous and just society. The libertarian philosophy envisioned a world where individuals were empowered to make their own choices and live according to their own values.

Libertarian means:

a. authoritarian   b. statistician   c. individualist

Ominous

As the dark clouds gathered overhead, casting a foreboding shadow over the landscape, an inauspicious sense of impending doom enveloped the town. The atmosphere became heavy with an air of uncertainty, and whispers of fear and unease spread through the community. Nature seemed to mirror the growing apprehension, as lightning streaked across the sky and thunder rumbled ominously in the distance.

Ominous means:

a. foreboding   b. reassuring   c. benign

Potent

In medicine, the scientist meticulously studied the potent compound, recognizing its immense power to elicit physiological changes within the human body. With its concentrated and robust properties, the substance held the potential to combat disease and alleviate suffering. Its potency, when harnessed wisely, could bring about groundbreaking advancements in medical treatment.

Potent means:

a. weak   b. feeble   c. powerful

Ruminate

Under the shade of a centuries-old oak tree, the poet sat in deep contemplation, allowing his thoughts to wander, meander, and ruminate. With each passing moment, he delved into the labyrinth of his mind, exploring memories, emotions, and ideas. He sought clarity and insight, paving the way for creative expression and self-discovery.

Ruminate means:

a. ponder   b. neglect   c. disregard

Transcribe

The diligent secretary tirelessly transcribed the complex dictations of the CEO, meticulously capturing every word to preserve the essence and intent of the message. With unwavering focus, she adeptly transferred the spoken words onto paper, ensuring accuracy and clarity in the written document. Her ability to document with precision and speed was instrumental in maintaining efficient communication within the organization.

Transcribe means:

a. erase   b. omit   c. record

Allay

In the midst of a brewing storm, the leader emerged before the crowd, his calm and composed demeanor serving to relieve the rising anxieties of the people. With empathetic words and a reassuring presence, he eased the fears and tensions that had permeated the atmosphere. His genuine compassion and guidance helped allay the concerns, instilling a sense of hope and trust among the populace.

Allay means:

a. intensify   b. alleviate   c. provoke

Byline

At the bottom of the newspaper article, nestled beneath the meticulously crafted prose, sat the byline—a testament to the diligent work of the journalist behind the story. It proudly displayed the name of the author, giving credit. The byline served as a badge of honor, a recognition of the writer's dedication and contribution to the field of journalism.

Byline means:

a. acknowledgment   b. anonymity   c. unaccredited

Demur

In the middle of the fervent debate, one voice chose to demur, expressing a hesitant reluctance to fully endorse or engage in the prevailing discourse. With thoughtful reservation, the individual considered the various arguments and implications carefully before voicing his respectful dissent. His demurral stemmed from a desire to encourage nuanced discussion and the exploration of alternative perspectives.

Demur means:

a. agree   b. consent   c. hesitate

Exacerbate

In a tense situation, a misjudged comment had the potential to exacerbate the already fragile relations between the parties involved. The inflammatory nature of the statement threatened to ignite further animosity and deepen the existing divide. It was imperative to exercise caution and engage in thoughtful dialogue to prevent further escalation of the conflict.

Exacerbate means:

a. worsen   b. alleviate   c. improve

Ignominious

The disgraced general slinked away from the battlefield, his once illustrious career ending in an ignominious defeat. The echoes of the crowd's scornful jeers followed him, compounding his sense of shame and humiliation. The tarnished legacy he left behind served as a cautionary tale, a reminder of the devastating consequences of overconfidence and hubris.

Ignominious means:

a. shameful   b. honorable   c. glorious

Liniment

With aching muscles and weary bones, the athlete eagerly reached for the soothing balm, applying it with practiced precision. The warming sensation offered relief, penetrating deep into the tired tissues and easing away the strains and pains accumulated through hours of training. The liniment became an indispensable companion, aiding in the athlete's recovery and maintaining optimal performance.

Liniment means:

a. ointment   b. irritant   c. abrasion

Omnipotent

The ancient deity loomed over the mortals, exuding a powerful aura that commanded both reverence and awe. With supreme power and authority, she shaped the very fabric of the world, her influence extending to the furthest reaches of existence. The mortals could only marvel at the unfathomable might and wisdom of the omnipotent being.

Omnipotent means:

a. almighty   b. powerless   c. feeble

Pragmatic

In the face of daunting challenges and complex problems, the pragmatic leader took a realistic approach to find effective solutions. Instead of getting caught up in abstract theories or unattainable ideals, he focused on what was achievable within the constraints of the situation. His pragmatic mindset allowed him to navigate obstacles and make sound decisions based on practicality and feasibility.

Pragmatic means:

a. theoretical   b. practical   c. idealistic

Ruse

The cunning detective devised an intricate ruse to deceive the elusive thieves, creating an elaborate web of deception that would lead them right into the trap. With meticulous attention to details, he orchestrated a series of carefully calculated moves, masquerading as an unsuspecting target. The final act of the maneuver would unfold in the darkened alleyway, where the detective lay in wait, ready to apprehend the criminal.

Ruse means:

a. deception   b. honesty   c. truth

Transgress

The young rebel, driven by a desire to challenge societal norms, dared to transgress the boundaries that had been imposed upon him. He defied the expectations and restrictions placed upon himself, forging ahead on a path of rebellion and self-discovery. However, the consequences of his actions remained to be seen, as he teetered on the precipice of uncertain outcomes.

Transgress means:

a. obey   b. violate   c. comply

Alleviate

In the middle of turmoil and suffering, an act of compassion had the power to ease the burdens weighing heavily upon the shoulders of those in need. With genuine empathy, the kind-hearted Samaritan offered a helping hand, seeking to alleviate the pain and hardships endured by their fellow human beings. Through small yet meaningful gestures, he ignited a glimmer of hope in the lives they touched.

Alleviate means:

a. relieve   b. worsen   c. intensify

Cacophony

The bustling city streets reverberated with a cacophony of sounds, a symphony of honking horns, bustling crowds, and street vendors calling out their wares. The chaotic medley of noise encompassed the vibrant energy of urban life, a rhapsody that both fascinated and overwhelmed the senses. Amidst the jumbled discord, a sense of harmony could still be found, hidden within the symphony of noise.

Cacophony means:

a. clamor   b. silence   c. tranquility

Denounce

In the face of injustice and oppression, the brave activist stood on the podium, ready to denounce the systemic biases that perpetuated the cycle of discrimination. With unwavering conviction, he exposed the flaws in the prevailing systems, condemning the actions and ideologies that enabled and perpetuated inequality. His impassioned denouncement served as a rallying cry for change and social progress.

Denounce means:

a. condemn   b. endorse   c. praise

Exasperated

The weary traveler, having encountered countless obstacles and setbacks, felt an overwhelming sense of annoyance seep into his bones. The continuous stream of challenges had tested his patience and resolve, leaving him longing for a respite from the arduous journey he had undertaken. However, the glimmer of hope still flickered within his heart, refusing to be extinguished by the weight of exasperation.

Exasperated means:

a. calm   b. irritated   c. patient

Ignominy

In politics, a single scandal has the power to forever tarnish a once revered figure, subjecting him to the ignominy of public shame and disgrace. The betrayals and wrongdoings of those entrusted with leadership can bring forth a wave of collective disappointment, forever eroding the trust placed in them. The path to redemption, if ever attainable, remains veiled in the shadows of dishonor.

Ignominy means:

a. disgrace   b. honor   c. dignity

Lithe

In the ballet studio, the lithe dancers moved with a graceful precision, their bodies flowing like liquid poetry across the polished floor. Every muscle and sinew worked in unison, creating a symphony of movement that captivated all who beheld it. The flexible dancers, like a swan on a tranquil lake, seemed to defy gravity itself in a mesmerizing display of lightness.

Lithe means:

a. inflexible   b. agile   c. clumsy

Omniscient

In the ancient myths and legends, the gods were often portrayed as omniscient beings, possessing an all-encompassing knowledge of the world and the fates of mortals. Their wisdom transcended human comprehension, guiding the destinies of those beneath them. The wise deities watched with knowing eyes as the mortal struggle unfolded, holding the answers to the mysteries of life and beyond.

Omniscient means:

a. all-knowing   b. ignorant   c. unaware

Pragmatist

Amidst the philosophical debates, the pragmatic thinkers sought practical solutions rather than engaging in abstract theoretical discussions. They saw value in taking action and implementing tangible strategies to address the challenges of everyday life. The pragmatists believed that the efficacy of an idea should be judged by its feasibility and its ability to produce real-world results.

Pragmatist means:

a. realistic   b. idealist   c. visionary

Saccharin

At the bakery, the confectioner created delicate pastries with a touch of sweetness, delighting the palates of those who indulged in their treats. The saccharin icing added a subtle sugary note to the already delectable desserts, elevating them to a realm of sugary satisfaction. Though some might find this flavor overpowering, for others, it was a little taste of heaven.

Saccharin means:

a. sweet   b. bitter   c. sour

Transient

In the bustling cityscape, people rushed from one place to another, searching for purpose amidst the constant flux of ephemeral encounters. The brief moments shared between strangers on crowded trains and busy avenues served as reminders of the nature of human connections. In this transient existence, it was the moments of genuine connection that provided solace and a momentary sense of belonging.

Transient means:

a. eternal   b. lasting   c. fleeting

Aloof

In the grand ballroom, the enigmatic figures stood aloof from the boisterous revelry, observing the swirling crowd with a detached air. Their extreme demeanor seemed to convey a sense of indifference, as if they were an island in a sea of mirthful chaos. It was clear that engaging with others was not their inclination, for their presence remained unyielding throughout the night.

Aloof means:

a. distant   b. sociable   c. engaging

Cajole

With a silver tongue and a persuasive charm, the politician sought to manipulate the wavering constituents into supporting their cause. He carefully selected his words, appealing to the hopes and aspirations of the audience, luring them into their web of promises. The art of cajoling, when executed skillfully, could bend even the strongest wills to the desired outcome.

Cajole means:

a. coax   b. deter   c. repel

Deplete

Years of reckless exploitation had taken its toll on the once lush forest, consuming its resources and leaving behind only a barren wasteland. The unrestrained actions of humanity had drained the land of its vitality, leaving a scar that would take decades to heal, if ever. The consequences of unchecked greed ultimately led to the depletion of the very lifeblood sustaining our planet.

Deplete means:

a. restore   b. exhaust   c. increase

Exceptionable

In the courtroom, the defense attorney meticulously laid out her case, scrutinizing every piece of evidence and testimony for any exceptionable inconsistencies. Her unwavering dedication to justice demanded a meticulous examination of every detail, as she sought the truth amidst a sea of ambiguity. Any exceptionable flaw could cast doubt on the entire proceedings, potentially altering the course of justice.

Exceptionable means:

a. acceptable   b. commendable   c. objectionable

Illuminate

As dusk settled over the ancient city, the soft glow of countless lanterns began to lighten up the narrow streets, casting an enchanting aura upon the cobblestones. The warm, golden light danced upon the faces of the townsfolk, bringing forth a sense of wonder and tranquility. The power of illumination not only dispelled the darkness but also kindled a sense of unity among the community.

Illuminate means:

a. dim   b. brighten   c. obscure

Livid

Clutching the crumpled letter in their trembling hands, the betrayed lover felt a surge of anger and betrayal like a wildfire igniting within. The once calm demeanor gave way to a livid expression, as fiery words spilled from his lips in a whirlwind of raw emotion. The pain of betrayal, now etched upon his face, reflected the depths of his anger and shattered trust.

Livid means:

a. furious   b. calm   c. composed

Onerous

The weight of responsibility settled upon the young entrepreneur's shoulders as he embarked on his ambitious venture. The intricate web of tasks that awaited him seemed onerous, requiring immense dedication and unwavering commitment. However, his determination and resilience pushed him forward, determined to overcome the daunting challenges that lay ahead.

Onerous means:

a. burdensome   b. easy   c. manageable

Preamble

Before delving into the heart of her argument, the lawyer began her speech with a carefully crafted preamble, setting the stage for the subsequent debate. The introductory statements outlined the key principles and objectives that guided her case, drawing the audience's attention to the pivotal issues at hand. The preamble acted as a foundation, laying the groundwork for a compelling argument.

Preamble means:

a. preface   b. postscript   c. epilogue

Sacrosanct

The ancient temple stood as a testament to the sacrosanct beliefs and traditions held by generations past. The hallowed grounds exuded an aura of reverence, as people approached with a sense of awe and humility. The rituals performed within those sacred walls served as a reminder of the sacred bond between humanity and the divine.

Sacrosanct means:

a. holy   b. profane   c. secular

Traverse

Through treacherous terrain and unforgiving weather, the intrepid explorers embarked on their journey to sail the uncharted peaks of the mountains. Their every step was calculated, navigating their way amidst the rugged landscape. With unwavering determination, they pressed forward, each footfall bringing them closer to the ultimate goal of traversing the formidable range.

Traverse means:

a. cross   b. stay   c. stagnate

Altruism

In a world often plagued by self-interest, the display of true altruism was a rare and precious gem. The selfless actions of individuals who put the well-being of others before their own stood as a testament to the beauty of the human spirit. The altruistic gestures, driven by compassion and empathy, had the power to ignite a chain reaction of kindness and goodwill.

Altruism means:

a. egotism   b. greed   c. selflessness

Caldron

Gathered around the flickering fire, the group of witches prepared their mystical brew within the ancient caldron. The bubbling cauldron contained a concoction of rare herbs and potions, each ingredient carefully chosen to produce the desired enchantment. As they chanted incantations, it emitted wisps of smoke, revealing the culmination of their magical endeavor.

Caldron means:

a. pot   b. flask   c. cup

Deplore

As news of the devastating circumstances reached the ears of the compassionate leaders, they couldn't help but deplore the profound suffering endured by the displaced refugees. The harrowing tales and desperate pleas painted a grim picture of despair, evoking a deep sense of sympathy within their heart. Despite the overwhelming challenges, they vowed to work tirelessly, determined to alleviate the onus of pain carried by those in need.

Deplore means:

a. praise   b. lament   c. applaud

Exculpate

In the dimly lit courtroom, the defense attorney presented a compelling argument, meticulously unravelling the intricacies of the case to exonerate his innocent client. With each piece of evidence and witness testimony, the attorney skillfully dismantled the illusion of guilt, shedding light on the true sequence of events. As the truth prevailed, the jury was left with no choice but to exculpate the accused.

Exculpate means:

a. acquit   b. condemn   c. accuse

Illusory

The allure of the magician's performance captivated the audience, who marveled at the illusions created before their very eyes. With deft movements and masterful sleight of hand, the magician skillfully crafted an unreal world, blurring the lines between reality and fantasy. However, as the show reached its climax, the audience realized the illusory nature of the tricks, leaving them in awe of the magician's artistry.

Illusory means:

a. deceptive   b. real   c. concrete

Lobbyist

Navigating the intricate corridors of power, the seasoned lobbyists tirelessly advocated for the interests of their clients, maneuvering through the political landscape with finesse. Armed with persuasive arguments and extensive research, they engaged in dialogue with lawmakers, seeking to influence legislation that aligned with their clients' objectives. Through strategic lobbying efforts, they aimed to shape policies in favor of those they represented.

Lobbyist means:

a. dissenter   b. critic   c. advocate

Onus

The weight of responsibility settled upon the shoulders of the young entrepreneurs as they embarked on their ambitious venture. They embraced the onus of success, knowing that their decisions and actions would directly impact the outcome of their business. Through determination and resilience, they navigated the challenges and obstacles, determined to carry the onus of building a thriving enterprise.

Onus means:

a. burden   b. privilege   c. option

Precarious

Perched on the edge of a steep cliff, the mountaineers carefully navigated the precarious path, aware that a single misstep could lead to dire consequences. The unstable terrain and unpredictable weather tested their skills and resilience, as they balanced on the precipice of danger. With careful calculation and unwavering focus, they successfully conquered the treacherous route, leaving behind the precariousness of the peak.

Precarious means:

a. stable   b. certain   c. uncertain

Sagacious

Within the ancient wisdom, the sagacious sage was revered for his profound intellect and discerning insights. With a wealth of knowledge amassed through years of study, his guidance was sought by kings and scholars alike. His sapient advice illuminated the path to enlightenment for all who sought his counsel.

Sagacious means:

a. wise   b. foolish   c. naïve

Trepidation

As the time approached for the daunting leap from the airplane, an overwhelming sense of anxiety gripped the skydiver's heart. The unknown heights and exhilarating free fall invoked a mix of fear and excitement, making the anticipation almost unbearable. However, with every ounce of courage, they overcame their trepidation and dived into the abyss, embracing the thrill of the experience.

Trepidation means:

a. assurance   b. apprehension   c. bravery

Amass

Through unwavering determination and ceaseless effort, the ambitious entrepreneur set out to collect a vast fortune, tirelessly navigating the competitive landscape of the business world. By capitalizing on innovative ideas and strategic partnerships, his empire grew exponentially, reaching unprecedented heights of success. His ability to amass wealth became a testament to his unwavering drive.

Amass means:

a. accumulate   b. disperse   c. squander

Callow

In the halls of higher education, the unfledged freshman found themselves surrounded by a diverse array of knowledge and experiences. With wide-eyed curiosity and a thirst for understanding, he embarked on his academic journey, eager to absorb all that the university had to offer. Gradually, he shed his callow nature, maturing into confident and knowledgeable scholars.

Callow means:

a. worldly   b. mature   c. inexperienced

Depravity

In the shadowed corners of society, a sinister figure reveled in the depths of human immorality, orchestrating acts of cruelty and malevolence. Through manipulation and coercion, she corrupted those who fell within her grasp, dragging them into a world devoid of morality. The web of depravity spun by this malefactor ensnared all who dared to venture too close.

Depravity means:

a. corruption   b. virtue   c. integrity

Execrable

The vile dictator's reign was marked by detestable acts of oppression and violence, as he callously trampled upon the rights and freedoms of his own citizens. The once-thriving nation was consumed by despair and misery, shackled by the chains of the tyrant's rule. The people yearned for liberation from the execrable grip of their oppressor.

Execrable means:

a. abominable   b. commendable   c. excellent

Immoderate

In a world of indulgence and excess, an unrestrained spender possessed an insatiable appetite for lavish extravagance. Whether it be acquiring opulent possessions or indulging in hedonistic pleasures, his insatiable desire knew no bounds. The consequences of his immoderate behavior soon caught up with him, leaving behind a trail of financial ruin and shattered relationships.

Immoderate means:

a. excessive   b. moderate   c. frugal

Lofty

Perched atop the majestic mountain peak, the mountaineers gazed upon the breathtaking vista that stretched out before them. The lofty peaks, kissed by the golden hues of the setting sun, seemed to touch the heavens themselves. In that moment, a profound sense of awe and wonder filled their heart, reminding them of the insignificance of their existence against the backdrop of nature's grandeur.

Lofty means:

a. majestic   b. lowly   c. humble

Opaque

Inmost the dense forest, sunlight struggled to pierce the thick canopy, casting an mirky veil over the woodland floor. Shadows danced amidst the foliage, obscuring the path ahead and lending an air of mystery to the ancient woods. Each step forward was a venture into the unknown, guided only by the faint sounds and fainter glimpses afforded by the opaque surroundings.

Opaque means:

a. murky   b. transparent   c. clear

Precedent

Throughout law and justice, every decision made by the court holds the weight of precedent, shaping the future course of legal interpretation. The principles established in previous cases set the foundation upon which the judicial system operates, ensuring consistency and fairness. Through the careful analysis of precedent, lawyers build persuasive arguments, seeking to sway the courts in their favor.

Precedent means:

a. exception   b. deviation   c. example

Sage

In the tranquil confines of the monastery, the venerable sage imparted his centuries of wisdom to eager disciples. Through profound contemplation and dedicated study, his mind had become a treasure trove of knowledge. His very words were like drops of nectar, nourishing the minds of his followers and inspiring them on their own paths to enlightenment.

Sage means:

a. foolish   b. wise   c. ignorant

Trinket

Inside the ornate jewelry box, nestled amongst the precious gemstones and gleaming gold, lay a simple trinket—a small, delicate pendant with sentimental value far surpassing its material worth. While it may have seemed insignificant to others, to its owner, it held memories of a cherished time and a bond that transcended the boundaries of materialism. The trinket served as a constant reminder of the love and connection shared with a dear friend.

Trinket means:

a. treasure   b. heirloom   c. knickknack

Ambiguity

Ambiguity is a literary technique employed by skilled writers to create layers of meaning and invite interpretation from the readers. Through carefully crafted words and subtle hints, the author weaves a narrative that dances on the fine edge of uncertainty, leaving room for multiple plausible interpretations. It is within the ambiguity that the readers' imagination is set free, allowing them to delve into the depths of the story and draw their own conclusions.

Ambiguity means:

a. vagueness   b. clarity   c. precision

Candid

In a world filled with superficiality and facade, a straightforward conversation can be a breath of fresh air. It is through the earnest and open exchange of thoughts and emotions that true connections are forged. A candid individual possesses a remarkable ability to speak his mind sincerely, unfiltered by societal expectations or personal agendas, and in doing so he lay the foundation for authentic relationships built on trust and understanding.

Candid means:

a. frank   b. deceitful   c. evasive

Deprecate

With every passing era, societal norms shift, and values evolve, rendering certain beliefs and practices obsolete. It is within this changing landscape that the act of deprecating outdated ideologies becomes imperative. As society progresses, it is essential to recognize and criticize ideas and actions that perpetuate harm or hinder progress. To deprecate is not to reject or dismiss one's cultural heritage but to acknowledge the need for growth and embrace a path towards a more inclusive future.

Deprecate means:

a. criticize   b. approve   c. praise

Exegesis

In biblical studies, scholars engage in exegesis, a meticulous process of rendition aimed at unraveling the deeper meanings embedded within sacred texts. It is through this scholarly endeavor that a thorough understanding of the historical contexts, cultural nuances, and spiritual insights can be gleaned from ancient scriptures. Exegesis requires a deep reverence for the texts and a commitment to the pursuit of knowledge.

Exegesis means:

a. misinterpretation   b. misunderstanding   c. interpretation

Immutable

Amidst the ever-changing tides of life, certain principles and laws remain constant, unyielding in their essence. These immutable truths provide a stable foundation upon which societies are built. While circumstances and individuals may change, the principles of justice, equality, and compassion stand as beacons, guiding humanity towards a harmonious existence. It is through embracing these timeless ideals that societies can hope to progress and flourish.

Immutable means:

a. unchangeable   b. changeable   c. flexible

Longevity

In our pursuit of a fulfilled existence, many seek not just a life well-lived but a life of longevity, filled with purpose and vitality. It extends beyond mere survival; it encompasses physical, mental, and emotional well-being. It is a testament to the resilience of the human spirit, the ability to adapt and thrive in the face of challenges, and the pursuit of a balanced lifestyle that nourishes both body and soul.

Longevity means:

a. transience   b. durability   c. brevity

Opulent

Nestled amidst the rolling hills, a grand mansion adorned with gilded chandeliers and intricate tapestries stood as a testament to lavishness. Its expansive halls echoed with whispers of the past, each room meticulously furnished with luxurious velvet drapes and ornate marble statues. The opulent estate exuded a sense of grandeur, reflecting the wealth and prosperity of its inhabitants.

Opulent means:

a. luxurious   b. modest   c. humble

Precept

Inside the hallowed halls of the monastery, the diligent monks devoted themselves to a life guided by timeless precepts. Etched in ancient scriptures and passed down through generations, these moral teachings served as a compass, steering individuals towards righteousness and enlightenment. The adherence to the precept of compassion fostered a spirit of kindness and empathy among the monks and paved the path towards spiritual awakening.

Precept means:

a. principle   b. disregard   c. violation

Salacious

In the dimly lit corner of the speakeasy, smoky tendrils entwined with laughter and whispered secrets. The air crackled with an undercurrent of desire as clandestine lovers indulged in salacious conversations, their voices veiled by secrecy. In this ephemeral haven of sensuality, inhibitions loosened, and the dance of temptation unfolded, leaving an air of excitement and illicit pleasure hanging in the atmosphere.

Salacious means:

a. modest   b. haste   c. lewd

Trite

With each passing year, the annual talent show seemed to lose its sparkle, the performances growing increasingly trite and predictable. The familiar melodies and worn-out routines failed to ignite the audience's enthusiasm, leaving them craving for originality and genuine artistic expression. It was time to break free from the confines of convention and redefine what it meant to captivate and inspire through the unexplored realms of creativity.

Trite means:

a. banal   b. original   c. fresh

Ambiguous

Ted stood at the crossroads of his life, torn between two paths, each shrouded in ambiguity. The future lay before him like an enigma, its possibilities intertwining and diverging, leaving him uncertain and contemplative. As he embarked on this journey of self-discovery, he vowed to embrace the ambiguity, for it held within it the potential for growth and revelation.

Ambiguous means:

a. vague   b. clear   c. definite

Candor

In the world of politics, where words are carefully chosen and public image meticulously crafted, a rare trait emerged: candor. The charismatic leader eschewed carefully scripted speeches and spoke from the heart, unafraid to voice unpopular opinions or tackle challenging issues head-on. The refreshing openness breathed life into a field plagued by empty promises and vague rhetoric, rekindling hope for a more transparent and accountable government.

Candor means:

a. deceit   b. honesty   c. evasion

Deride

He stood on the stage, vulnerable yet determined, presenting his innovative idea to the skeptical crowd. Their smirks and mocking whispers pierced his confidence, but he refused to be deterred. With unwavering conviction, he continued, knowing that one day his work would prove them wrong, and their derisive laughter would transform into awe.

Deride means:

a. ridicule   b. admire   c. praise

Exemplary

Amidst the chaos of war, a solitary soldier emerged as an embodiment of bravery and selflessness. With each act of heroism, he exemplified the values of honor and sacrifice. His unwavering dedication to his comrades and his exemplary commitment to his mission were unparalleled, leaving an indelible mark on the annals of history.

Exemplary means:

a. admirable   b. flawed   c. mediocre

Impartial

The judge solemnly presided over the courtroom, her impartiality evident in every decision she made. She listened intently, weighing the evidence with meticulous attention to detail. Free from personal biases, her commitment to justice ensured that each verdict was fair and just, restoring faith in the legal system.

Impartial means:

a. unbiased   b. partial   c. unfair

Loquacious

In the bustling café, her voice soared above the clatter of coffee cups and lively conversations. She regaled her friends with animated anecdotes and witty remarks, her loquacious nature captivating the room. Her exuberant energy and gift for storytelling made her the life of the party.

Loquacious means:

a. talkative   b. quiet   c. taciturn

Ordain

The temple was abuzz with anticipation as the high priest prepared to ordain the young acolyte. With ancient rituals and sacred chants, he blessed him with wisdom and bestowed upon him the mantle of spiritual leadership. The congregation gathered, their hearts filled with hope and reverence for this auspicious occasion.

Ordain means:

a. consecrate   b. dismiss   c. abolish

Precinct

In the heart of the city, the bustling precinct pulsated with life. Neon lights illuminated the busy streets, casting a kaleidoscope of colors on the pavement. Shops, restaurants, and theaters lined the precinct, inviting visitors to indulge in a world filled with endless possibilities.

Precinct means:

a. district   b. outskirts   c. countryside

Sallow

The weary traveler crossed the arid desert, her face bearing the marks of exhaustion and dehydration. Her once radiant complexion had faded, leaving behind a sallow shade that mirrored the barren landscape. She longed for a sip of cool water to quench her parched throat and restore vitality to her pallid features.

Sallow means:

a. wan   b. vibrant   c. rosy

Trivial

In the grand tapestry of human existence, he pondered the significance of his everyday actions. The weight of trivial decisions burdened his mind, questioning the purpose behind each choice. Lost in a sea of inconsequential concerns, he yearned for a deeper sense of meaning in a world that often trivialized the profound.

Trivial means:

a. significant   b. minor   c. substantial

Ambivalence

She stood at the crossroads of life, torn between two divergent paths. Hesitation gripped her heart as she weighed the pros and cons, unable to commit to either choice. The weight of uncertainty hovered over her, threatening to stifle her progress until she found the courage to embrace one path and leave ambivalence behind.

Ambivalence means:

a. indecision   b. certainty   c. conviction

Cantankerous

The old man sat on his porch, his grizzled face mirroring the cranky nature that defined him. He bellowed and scowled at any passerby who dared to interrupt his isolation. Resentful of the world, his acerbic remarks and bitter demeanor exemplified the depth of his cantankerous disposition.

Cantankerous means:

a. grumpy   b. amiable   c. pleasant

Derogatory

The classroom fell silent as the teacher sternly admonished the student for his offensive comments. The weight of his hurtful words echoed through the room, staining the atmosphere with negativity. Through disciplinary action, the teacher sought to remind the student of the importance of respectful dialogue and the consequences of derogatory language.

Derogatory means:

a. disparaging   b. praise   c. admiring

Exemplify

At the heart of the bustling city, the grand library exemplified the pursuit of knowledge. Its towering architecture and vast collection of books paid homage to centuries of intellectual inquiry. Visitors from all walks of life flocked to its hallowed halls, seeking wisdom and enlightenment.

Exemplify means:

a. represent   b. deviate   c. contradict

Impecunious

In the quaint village nestled amidst rolling hills, lived a family whose meager earnings could barely sustain their basic needs. Their impecunious condition compelled them to make sacrifices and live a frugal life, devoid of luxury or extravagance. Yet, amidst their financial struggles, they cherished the priceless bonds of love and resilience that held them together.

Impecunious means:

a. affluent   b. penniless   c. wealthy

Lucid

The esteemed professor captivated his students with his coherent explanations, unraveling complex theories with remarkable clarity. His eloquent language and logical progression of ideas painted a vivid mental landscape, enabling even the most abstract concepts to take shape in the minds of his eager learners. Through his teachings, they glimpsed the beauty of lucid thought and the power of effective communication.

Lucid means:

a. clear   b. vague   c. confusing

Ornate

The grand ballroom shimmered under the golden chandeliers, adorned with intricate carvings and elaborate designs. Every detail spoke of the extravagant opulence that characterized the era, from the gilded framed mirrors to the finely embroidered tapestries that graced the walls. Guests, dressed in their finest attire, reveled in the grandeur of an evening that epitomized the essence of ornate elegance.

Ornate means:

a. lavish   b. plain   c. understated

Precipice

Standing on the edge of the jagged cliff, he felt a mix of exhilaration and fear as he gazed into the abyss below. The sheer drop seemed to beckon him, tempting him to take a leap of faith into the unknown. However, his rational mind alerted him to the dangers lurking at the precipice, reminding him of the importance of caution and calculated decision-making.

Precipice means:

a. brink   b. foundation   c. base

Salubrious

In Shanghai, a bustling city, a small park offered a tranquil retreat, its lush greenery and fragrant blossoms providing a salubrious oasis amidst the concrete jungle. The crisp, clean air invigorated both body and mind, rejuvenating weary souls seeking respite from the hectic pace of urban life. It was a sanctuary where one could indulge in the salubrious effects of nature's healing touch.

Salubrious means:

a. healthy   b. harmful   c. unhealthy

Truant

In the hallowed halls of learning, was a student whose rebellious spirit led him astray. He wandered aimlessly through the streets, evading the structured confines of the school, embracing the freedom that truancy brought. Yet, unbeknownst to him, the consequences of his wayward choices loomed ever closer, threatening to shatter his dreams and corrode his potential.

Truant means:

a. delinquent   b. punctual   c. diligent

Ambulatory

The medieval cathedral stood tall, its ambulatory ablaze with the golden hues of sunlight filtering through intricately stained glass windows. As visitors meandered through the winding corridors, they marveled at the architectural marvels and revered artworks that adorned the mobile, encapsulating centuries of religious devotion and artistic ingenuity. The tranquil aura of the space enveloped them, leaving an indelible impression of reverence and tranquility.

Ambulatory means:

a. walking

b. stationary

c. immobile

Capacious

In the expansive gallery, the capacious walls provided a vast canvas for renowned artists to display their masterpieces. The sheer scale of the space allowed for the exhibition of large-scale sculptures and immersive installations. Visitors were awestruck by the capaciousness of the gallery, as it accommodated a diverse range of art forms and offered ample room for introspection and interpretation.

Capacious means:

a. spacious

b. cramped

c. narrow

Desecrate

In a world where reverence and sanctity were cherished, the profanation of a sacred temple sent shockwaves through the community. The once pristine halls were now marred by graffiti and shattered relics, a heart-wrenching sight that struck at the core of believers' faith. The desecration of such a revered space stood as a somber reminder of the consequences when irreverence defiles the sacred.

Desecrate means:

a. defile

b. honor

c. revere

Exhaustive

The dedicated scientist diligently undertook a complete study, meticulously examining every minute detail and leaving no stone unturned. Countless hours were spent in the laboratory, tirelessly conducting experiments and analyzing data to ensure a comprehensive understanding of the subject. The resulting research paper stood as a testament to the exhaustive pursuit of knowledge and the thirst for scientific breakthroughs.

Exhaustive means:

a. cursory

b. partial

c. thorough

Impious

In the serene halls of the ancient monastery, whispered prayers and sacred chants reverberated, their faithful echoes resonating with piety and devotion. However, an impious visitor disrupted the sanctity of this holy refuge, mocking the rituals and displaying a lack of reverence. The blasphemy hung in the air, a breach of trust that left the devout souls bewildered and saddened.

Impious means:

a. irreverent   b. pious   c. reverent

Ludicrous

In the theater of absurdity, actors donned outlandish costumes and delivered lines that defied logic, inviting uproarious laughter from the audience. The ridiculous plot twists and exaggerated theatrics drew gales of mirth, suspending disbelief and embracing the delightful chaos of the stage. The final act revealed the true extent of the ludicrous comedy, leaving the spectators in stitches and applauding with joy.

Ludicrous means:

a. sensible   b. logical   c. absurd

Orthodox

In the ancient monastery, the devout monks upheld the traditions that had endured for centuries, adhering strictly to the established rituals and doctrines. Their unwavering commitment to these practices shaped their lives, fostering a deep connection to the divine and nurturing their spiritual growth. The wisdom and guidance of the orthodox teachings provided solace and direction to those seeking enlightenment.

Orthodox means:

a. traditional   b. heretical   c. unorthodox

Precipitous

As the intrepid mountaineer ascended the treacherous peak, the path became increasingly abrupt, with jagged cliffs and sheer drops challenging every step. The heart-stopping views from such precipitous heights were awe-inspiring, evoking a sense of exhilaration mixed with a tinge of fear. With each cautious maneuver, the mountaineer pushed their limits, conquering the landscape with unwavering determination.

Precipitous means:

a. steep   b. gradual   c. gentle

Salutary

In the face of adversity, the wise sage offered incredible advice, imbuing hope and wisdom in the hearts of those who sought solace. The salutary words brought clarity to the bewildered minds, offering a path forward amidst turmoil and uncertainty. Through his guidance, individuals emerged stronger, armed with newfound resilience and a refreshed perspective on life's challenges.

Salutary means:

a. harmful b. beneficial c. deleterious

Truncate

The acclaimed novelist made the bold decision to abbreviate the final chapters of the epic saga, leaving readers in suspense and igniting passionate debates about the characters' fates. The masterful use of the truncate technique heightened the narrative tension, intensifying readers' curiosity and anticipation. While some yearned for a more conclusive ending, others appreciated the artistic choice to truncate, as it allowed for personal interpretations and open-ended possibilities.

Truncate means:

a. shorten b. extend c. elongate

Ameliorate

In the impoverished village, the arrival of humanitarian aid improved the dire living conditions, offering a glimmer of hope and a chance for a better future. The provision of food, clean water, and medical supplies ameliorated the immediate hardships, providing a temporary respite from suffering. The collective efforts to alleviate the villagers' lives ignited a spark of optimism, encouraging them to strive for lasting change.

Ameliorate means:

a. worsen b. deteriorate c. enhance

Capitulate

After a long and grueling battle, the outnumbered troops were left with no choice but to surrender to the enemy's superior might. The decision to capitulate was a painful one, for it meant relinquishing their freedom and succumbing to the yoke of oppression. However, the brave soldiers clung to the hope that one day, they would rise again and reclaim their independence.

Capitulate means:

a. yield b. defy c. resist

Desecration

Huddled in the shadow of the ancient temple, the archaeologists were appalled to discover the profanation that had befallen the sacred site. The senseless defilement of the revered sanctuary, with its broken statues and vandalized murals, filled their hearts with anguish and outrage. The desecration of this historical treasure was a tragic reminder of humanity's capacity for destruction and disregard for cultural heritage.

Desecration means:

a. violation   b. sanctity   c. reverence

Exonerates

In a stunning turn of events, new evidence emerged that absolved the wrongfully accused prisoner, casting doubt on his guilt and unraveling the flawed conviction. The meticulously gathered testimonies and forensic analysis conclusively exonerated the individual, shedding light on his innocence and exposing the flaws within the justice system. As the truth prevailed, the exoneration brought not only solace to the innocent, but also a renewed scrutiny of the mechanisms that led to his wrongful imprisonment.

Exonerates means:

a. acquits   b. implicates   c. accuses

Impoverished

On the outskirts of the gleaming metropolis, hidden from the glaring lights, lay a destitute neighborhood where impoverished families struggled to survive amidst scarcity and deprivation. The harsh reality of their daily existence, chiseled by hunger and hardship, stood in stark contrast to the opulence of the surrounding city. The pervasive poverty that hung in the air suffocated their dreams and aspirations, leaving them trapped in an unyielding cycle of pauperisation.

Impoverished means:

a. affluent   b. wealthy   c. needy

Lukewarm

As the warm water cascaded down her body, she found no respite from the stifling summer heat. The warm streams failed to invigorate her senses, leaving her longing for the refreshing embrace of cooler temperatures. The lukewarm temperatures persisted, neither providing the comfort of warmth nor the relief of coolness, leaving her in a state of perpetual discomfort.

Lukewarm means:

a. tepid   b. hot   c. fervent

Ossify

With each passing year, the once agile dancer began to notice the subtle changes in her body as age started to ossify her joints and limbs. The fluid grace that once defined her movements began to fade, replaced by a rigidity that hindered her artistry. The process of ossification served as a poignant reminder of the impermanence of youth and the relentless march of time.

Ossify means:

a. harden　　　　　　　　b. loosen　　　　　　　　c. soften

Preclude

The implementation of strict security measures precluded any unauthorized access to the top-secret research facility, ensuring the confidentiality of classified information and protecting the integrity of groundbreaking discoveries. The impenetrable barriers, armed guards, and sophisticated surveillance systems hindered even the most determined intruders from breaching the facility's defenses. The fortifications in place precluded any compromise to the invaluable research conducted within those secure walls.

Preclude means:

a. allow　　　　　　　　b. prevent　　　　　　　　c. enable

Sanctimonious

The preacher's sermon dripped with rhetoric, as he pontificated from the pulpit about the virtues of holiness and piety. His pious proclamations, laced with moral superiority, elicited both admiration and suspicion from the congregation who questioned the genuineness behind his words. In the end, his actions revealed the true nature of his sanctimonious façade.

Sanctimonious means:

a. sincere　　　　　　　　b. modest　　　　　　　　c. self-righteous

Tumult

In the bustling city square, a ceaseless uproar of voices and activity engulfed every corner, giving rise to a cacophony of sounds and a dizzying array of sights. Street vendors called out their wares, couples strolled hand in hand, and the occasional honking of car horns added to the relentless turmoil. Amidst the chaos, she found solace in the tranquil park, seeking respite from the tumult of everyday life.

Tumult means:

a. commotion　　　　　　　　b. calm　　　　　　　　c. silence

Amelioration

Through dedicated efforts and compassionate initiatives, the community witnessed a gradual betterment of the living conditions that had long plagued their neighborhood. Dilapidated buildings were renovated, education programs were established, and accessible healthcare services were provided, marking a significant advance in the quality of life for residents. The collective efforts of the community brought about a much-needed amelioration to their once challenging circumstances.

Amelioration means:
a. improvement   b. deterioration   c. worsening

Carping

The critics, ever eager to disparage and find fault, never missed an opportunity to indulge in their carping remarks about the acclaimed artist's latest masterpiece. Their critical scrutiny exposed their inability to appreciate the artist's unique vision and skill, reducing their critiques to mere trivialities. Undeterred by the carping voices, the artist continued to create, knowing that true art transcends the limitations of narrow-minded criticism.

Carping means:
a. nitpicking   b. applauding   c. praising

Desist

Knowing the consequences that awaited him, he made the difficult decision to abstain from his illicit activities, realizing that the path he had chosen would only lead to destruction and despair. With a heavy heart, he bid farewell to the dangerous world that had ensnared him for far too long, determined to forge a new, righteous path. His resolve to desist from his previous lifestyle was met with a newfound sense of liberation and hope.

Desist means:
a. pursue   b. stop   c. continue

Exorcism

The tormented souls sought solace in the ancient ritual of exorcism, hoping to banish the malevolent spirits that had plagued their existence. With fervent prayers and incantations, the exorcist invoked divine intervention, casting out the dark forces that had taken hold. As the ritual reached its crescendo, a profound sense of relief washed over the individuals, as they finally found liberation from the torment that had consumed them.

Exorcism means:
a. purification   b. possession   c. embrace

Impromptu

With eloquence and charm, the renowned pianist took to the stage and dazzled the audience with an improvised performance that showcased his extraordinary talent. The harmonious melodies resonated through the concert hall, captivating the listeners who were amazed by his ability to create such exquisite music on the spot. The impromptu recital left an indelible mark on the hearts of all those fortunate enough to witness it.

Impromptu means:

a. spontaneous   b. planned   c. prepared

Lummox

His towering stature and clumsy demeanor earned him the nickname "Lummox" among his friends. Despite his endearing awkwardness, he possessed a heart of gold, always willing to lend a helping hand. His friends cherished his presence, knowing that behind this label lay a loyal and gentle soul.

Lummox means:

a. oaf   b. graceful   c. agile

Ostentatious

Adorned in extravagant attire and dripping with opulent jewelry, the socialite arrived at the gala with a pretentious display of wealth and status. Every step she took exuded an air of superiority, as if she were the center of the universe. However, beneath the layers of pomp and grandeur, the emptiness of her ostentatious facade became increasingly apparent.

Ostentatious means:

a. showy   b. discreet   c. humble

Precocious

The talented child astounded her teachers and peers with her exceptional intellect and advanced comprehension far beyond her years. At a tender age, she tackled complex mathematical equations effortlessly and delved into philosophical debates with a maturity that belied her youth. Her precocious abilities marked her as a young prodigy destined for great achievements.

Precocious means:

a. average   b. gifted   c. normal

Sanction

In an official proclamation, the government declared its sanction upon the activities deemed illegal, urging citizens to abide by the law. The weight of the law's warrant loomed over transgressors, reminding them of the consequences that awaited those who dared to defy authority. It served as a powerful deterrent, maintaining social order and promoting compliance.

Sanction means:

a. approval   b. ban   c. prohibition

Turpitude

The heinous crimes committed by the corrupt politician left a stain on his legacy, exposing the depths of his moral turpitude. The web of deceit and manipulation he wove resulted in the suffering of countless innocent lives. The trial revealed the true extent of his corruption, further cementing his place in the annals of infamy.

Turpitude means:

a. depravity   b. integrity   c. decency

Amiable

Known for his amiable disposition and warm smile, Mr. Thompson was a beloved figure in the small town. His cheerful greetings and genuine interest in others made him a source of comfort and reassurance to those who crossed his path. Whether engaging in lively conversations or offering a helping hand, he left an indelible impression of kindness and goodwill.

Amiable means:

a. affable   b. hostile   c. aloof

Cartographer

Armed with a trusty compass and a keen eye for detail, the skilled cartographer embarked on a journey to map the uncharted territories. With steady hands, she carefully traced the contours of the land, meticulously recording every mountain peak and riverbed. Her intricate maps became invaluable tools for explorers and adventurers seeking to navigate the unknown.

Cartographer means:

a. mapmaker   b. navigator   c. explorer

Despondent

In the depths of despair, Sarah found herself in a gloomy state, overwhelmed by a suffocating sense of sadness. The weight of her shattered dreams pressed heavily upon her shoulders, casting a bleak shadow over her spirit. However, through the support of loved ones and resilience found within, she discovered the strength to rise above her despondency.

Despondent means:

a. dejected

b. optimistic

c. hopeful

Expatriate

Leaving behind familiar faces and the comforting embrace of home, John embraced a life as an expatriate in a foreign land. With a mixture of excitement and trepidation, he immersed himself in a new culture, eager to embrace the diversity and challenges that awaited him. As he built new relationships and adapted to his new surroundings, John discovered a newfound sense of belonging.

Expatriate means:

a. emigrant

b. native

c. resident

Inadvertent

With an accidental slip of the knife, the chef accidentally added an extra dash of spice to the simmering broth. Little did he know that this unintended addition would transform the dish into a culinary delight, elevating its flavors to new heights. Through his inadvertent mistake, he stumbled upon a serendipitous culinary innovation.

Inadvertent means:

a. deliberately

b. accidental

c. intentionally

Luscious

Beneath the sun-kissed orchard, rows upon rows of luscious fruits beckoned the passersby with their vibrant hues and tantalizing aromas. The succulent peaches, bursting with sweetness, seemed to whisper promises of bliss with every bite. Nature's bounty, in all its glory, served as a reminder of the exquisite beauty that can be found in the simplest of pleasures.

Luscious means:

a. delicious

b. bland

c. tasteless

Oust

Amidst the political turmoil, the young and ambitious candidate sought to dethrone his opponent from the coveted position of power. Through a strategic campaign, he eloquently articulated his vision for change, capturing the hearts and minds of the disillusioned masses. With a resounding victory at the polls, he successfully ousted his predecessor, heralding a new era of progress and leadership.

Oust means:

a. remove   b. retain   c. keep

Predecessor

As the new CEO of the company, Jennifer studied the successes and missteps of her predecessor with unwavering focus. She delved into the archives, poring over financial reports and analyzing past strategies to inform her own approach to leadership. Armed with invaluable insights, Jennifer was determined to build upon the foundation laid by her esteemed predecessor.

Predecessor means:

a. forerunner   b. successor   c. follower

Sanguinary

The battlefield, once a site of tranquility, became a sanguinary realm where bravery and sacrifice coalesced. The clash of metal against metal and the piercing cries of soldiers echoed through the blood-soaked field. Despite the horrors witnessed, the human spirit shone through the darkness, as tales of bravery and comradeship emerged from this butcherly chapter of history.

Sanguinary means:

a. bloody   b. peaceful   c. nonviolent

Tyro

In the hallowed halls of the conservatory, the young pianist stood before a discerning audience, eager to prove her worth as a tyro in the world of classical music. With trembling hands, she began to play, channeling her passion and unwavering dedication into every delicate note. The audience, captivated by her raw talent and determination, erupted into thunderous applause.

Tyro means:

a. expert   b. veteran   c. novice

Amity

In a world plagued by division and animosity, the diplomatic efforts between nations aimed to foster peace and understanding. Through dialogue and mutual respect, they sought to bridge the gaps that had long fueled conflict and mistrust. As the seeds of amity were sown, a glimmer of hope emerged, promising a brighter and more harmonious future.

Amity means:

a. friendship   b. enmity   c. discord

Castigate

With stern authority, the teacher reprimanded the unruly student for his disruptive behavior, emphasizing the importance of discipline and respect within the classroom. The cutting words penetrated the student's ego, leaving him humbled and remorseful. However, as the dust settled, the teacher's intention to castigate became clear: to instill a sense of accountability and foster personal growth.

Castigate means:

a. criticize   b. praise   c. commend

Destitution

In the heart of the city, amidst the towering skyscrapers and bustling streets, a figure cloaked in destitution wandered aimlessly. The burden of impoverishment weighed heavily upon him, stripping away his dignity and eroding his hope. Society turned a blind eye to his plight, leaving him trapped in the depths of destitution, desperately yearning for a glimmer of compassion.

Destitution means:

a. affluence   b. wealth   c. poverty

Expedient

Faced with an imminent crisis, the leaders of the nation were compelled to make tough decisions in the name of pragmatism. They weighed the short-term gains against the long-term consequences, navigating the treacherous waters of political expediency. Though the path they chose may have been expedient, it left a stain on their moral compass and raised questions about the true cost of their actions.

Expedient means:

a. impractical   b. beneficial   c. unwise

Incantation

Deep in the depths of the ancient forest, a cloaked figure whispered mystical incantations to summon the spirits from beyond. The air crackled with anticipation as the chant reached its crescendo, revealing glimpses of magic and mystery. His power granted him the ability to manipulate the forces of nature, unlocking a world previously unseen.

Incantation means:

a. spell   b. silence   c. hush

Lynch

In a small town plagued by bigotry and hatred, a mob formed with intentions to lynch an innocent man accused of a crime he did not commit. The frenzied crowd, fueled by prejudice and blind rage, sought to take justice into their own hands. As the mob closed in, the true test of justice and humanity lay in whether they would succumb to their savage instincts or rise above the brutality of an execution.

Lynch means:

a. hang   b. protect   c. save

Overt

The politician's true motives were cunningly veiled beneath a facade of charm and charisma, but his actions betrayed an apparent desire for power and control. Each move he made, carefully orchestrated to incrementally further his agenda, lacked subtlety or discretion. The electorate, slowly awakening to his overt manipulations, questioned whether they had been swept up in a grand illusion.

Overt means:

a. covert   b. hidden   c. obvious

Predicament

Caught in a web of deceit and betrayal, the protagonist found themselves in a precarious predicament, teetering on the edge of ruin. Every decision seemed to lead to further complications, entangling them in a seemingly endless maze of consequences. As the walls closed in, only a stroke of ingenuity could extricate them from their dire plight.

Predicament means:

a. dilemma   b. solution   c. resolution

Sanguine

In the face of adversity, she remained remarkably sanguine, her spirit undeterred by the challenges that lay ahead. With resolute optimism, she embraced the belief that better days would come, infusing hope into every step she took. Her unwavering resolve served as a beacon of light, illuminating the path to a brighter future.

Sanguine means:

a. helpful

b. pessimistic

c. gloomy

Ubiquitous

In today's modern society, technology has become ubiquitous, seamlessly integrating into every aspect of our lives. From the moment we wake up to the time we lay our heads to rest, its presence is undeniable. The ubiquity of technology has reshaped the way we communicate, learn, and navigate the world around us.

Ubiquitous means:

a. rare

b. limited

c. omnipresent

Amorphous

The concept of beauty is indefinite, transcending conventional definitions and boundaries. Its essence is fluid, defying rigid categorization. What one perceives as beauty may differ vastly from another's interpretation, resulting in an amorphous understanding that embraces diverse perspectives.

Amorphous means:

a. structured

b. shapeless

c. defined

Catharsis

Through the power of art, the poet sought comfort, a release of pent-up emotions that had long plagued her soul. As her verses poured onto the blank page, she felt a weight lifting, as if the burdens of the world were lifted from her shoulders. The catharsis she experienced through her craft brought solace and healing.

Catharsis means:

a. purification

b. inhibition

c. suppression

Deter

The haunting tales of the dangers lurking in the deep sea did little to deter the intrepid explorer from embarking on her maritime quest. The allure of the unknown and the promise of hidden wonders motivated her to face any obstacle that crossed her path. No admonitions or warnings could deter her from her relentless pursuit of discovery.

Deter means:

a. entice   b. discourage   c. encourage

Expedite

With time running short, the team put forth their best efforts to hasten the completion of the project. Every member poured their energy and expertise into the task at hand, ensuring minimal delays. Their coordinated efforts and precise execution expedited the process, allowing them to meet the deadline with time to spare.

Expedite means:

a. accelerate   b. delay   c. hinder

Incarceration

Within the cold, unforgiving walls of the penitentiary, time seemed to stretch infinitely for the souls bound by incarceration. Stripped of their freedom, each day blended into the next, suffocating their spirits with a profound sense of confinement. It was only in the dreams of a life beyond the prison gates that a glimmer of hope emerged, piercing through the despair that lingered in every corner.

Incarceration means:

a. liberation   b. freedom   c. confinement

Machinations

Behind closed doors, hidden from the prying eyes of the world, the intricate complots of power unfolded. With calculated precision, the puppet master pulled the strings, orchestrating a delicate dance of manipulation and deceit. His grand schemes, woven with a tapestry of political intrigue, sought to shape the destinies of nations and secure his own preeminent positions.

Machinations means:

a. schemes   b. transparency   c. openness

Overwrought

Her emotions, like a tempestuous storm, roiled within her, rendering her overwrought with anxiety and anguish. Each thought and feeling collided, creating a chaotic whirlwind of apprehension. Her mind, weary from the constant battle against inner turmoil, longed for a moment of respite and soothe her troubled soul.

Overwrought means:

a. calm   b. agitated   c. composed

Preeminent

In the world of academia, he stood as preeminent, revered for his unparalleled knowledge and groundbreaking research. His intellectual prowess and unwavering dedication had earned him respect among his peers and students alike. His contributions to his field were undeniably profound, solidifying his place as a true pioneer.

Preeminent means:

a. eminent   b. ordinary   c. mediocre

Sardonic

With a sardonic grin etched across his face, he delivered his cutting remarks, dripping with mocking sarcasm. His sharp wit pierced through the pretenses of those around him, exposing the hypocrisy embedded in their words and actions. His words were a double-edged sword, leaving his targets wounded but unable to resist a bitter chuckle.

Sardonic means:

a. sarcastic   b. sincere   c. genuine

Unalloyed

Their love was unalloyed, unclouded and untainted by the complications that often shadowed relationships. It resonated with an authenticity that transcended time and distance. Through life's trials, their bond remained unbreakable, a shining example of unwavering devotion that inspired all who witnessed it.

Unalloyed means:

a. pure   b. mixed   c. adulterated

Maelstrom

Caught in the relentless grip of a maelstrom, the ship was tossed about like a mere plaything of the tempestuous sea. The furious currents, swirling with an indomitable force, threatened to consume the vessel and its hapless crew. Desperation clung to their hearts as they fought against the overwhelming power of the storm, praying for a glimmer of salvation.

Maelstrom means:

a. whirlpool   b. calm   c. serenity

Palatable

The aroma wafting from the kitchen greeted them with an enticing promise of a palatable feast. With every carefully crafted dish, the chef transformed humble ingredients into a symphony of flavors that danced upon their tongues. The harmony of tastes and textures, meticulously balanced, made each bite a true culinary delight.

Palatable means:

a. distasteful   b. unpleasant   c. delicious

Prerogative

As the leader of the council, it was his prerogative to shape the future of their society. With careful consideration, he pondered the choices before him, aware of the weight that rested upon his shoulders. With great power came great responsibility, and his decisions would determine the path of their collective destiny.

Prerogative means:

a. limitation   b. right   c. constraint

Savant

Hidden within the recesses of his mind lay the brilliance of a savant. His prodigious intellect, beyond comprehension for most, allowed him to unravel the complexities of the universe. Science, mathematics, and art melded effortlessly in his thoughts, revealing a depth of knowledge that illuminated the world around him.

Savant means:

a. genius   b. dullard   c. simpleton

Unctuous

With a disarming smile plastered across his face, he delivered his unctuous compliments, each word coated in insincere charm. His oily demeanor, designed to win favor, left a residue of unease in the hearts of those who saw through his façade. Beneath the smooth surface of his flattery lay a calculated agenda.

Unctuous means:

a. oily

b. sincere

c. honest

Analogous

Just as the delicate wings of a butterfly mirrored the vibrant hues of a blooming flower, their destinies were intimately analogous. Threads of fate intertwined their lives, guiding them along parallel paths toward a shared destiny. The journey, though distinct in its particulars, echoed with a harmonious resonance.

Analogous means:

a. different

b. distinct

c. similar

Caustic

Her words lashed out like caustic venom, leaving a bitter taste in the air. With each sentence, she tore down their spirits, corroding their confidence with relentless criticism. The toxic nature of her remarks eroded the bonds of friendship, leaving only scars of resentment and pain.

Caustic means:

a. corrosive

b. gentle

c. soothing

Detrimental

The long-term consequences of his reckless actions proved to be detrimental to his well-being. Like a poison coursing through his veins, his self-destructive choices hindered his progress and shattered his dreams. The realization of the damage inflicted upon himself and those around him weighed heavily on his heart.

Detrimental means:

a. harmful

b. beneficial

c. helpful

Extol

With fervent admiration, they extolled the virtues of their beloved mentor. His wisdom and guidance illuminated their path, igniting a fire within their souls. Their voices rose in unison, praising his remarkable achievements and profound insights.

Extol means:

a. condemn
b. criticize
c. praise

Incipient

In the quiet stillness of the early morning, the incipient rays of the rising sun cast a soft glow upon the world. With each passing moment, the darkness relinquished its hold, giving way to the promise of a new day. Nature awakened from its slumber, hinting at the birth of endless possibilities.

Incipient means:

a. beginning
b. advanced
c. mature

Magnanimous

With a magnanimous gesture, he extended a helping hand to his fallen rival. Beneath the fierce competition and rivalries, he recognized the common struggle they shared. Setting aside his personal triumph, he chose to uplift and inspire, embodying the true spirit of sportsmanship.

Magnanimous means:

a. stingy
b. selfish
c. generous

Palisade

The towering palisade stood as a formidable barrier, guarding the ancient fortress. Its sturdy wooden structure, a testament to human ingenuity, boasted impenetrable walls and fortified defenses. Behind its protective embrace, the inhabitants found solace in the shelter it provided.

Palisade means:

a. fence
b. opening
c. entrance

Prescient

In a remarkable display of foresight, she predicted the impending economic downturn long before it gripped the nation. Her keen intellect and extensive research allowed her to discern patterns and anticipate outcomes with remarkable accuracy. Her prescient analysis proved invaluable to individuals seeking to safeguard their financial futures.

Prescient means:

a. insightful

b. shortsighted

c. oblivious

Scale

As the fire ravaged the forest, its destructive force grew exponentially, consuming everything in its path. The sheer scale of the inferno overwhelmed the efforts of the firefighters, as the flames danced higher, licking the sky with their fiery tongues. The devastation left behind was a testament to the relentless power of nature.

Scale means:

a. magnitude

b. miniature

c. smallness

Undermined

The constant stream of rumors and gossip gradually undermined the foundation of their once strong relationship. Doubt seeped in through the cracks, eroding the trust and nurturing seeds of suspicion. Despite their best efforts to mend the fractures, the damage done could not be undone.

Undermined means:

a. weaken

b. strengthen

c. bolster

Anarchy

In the absence of a governing body, pandemonium reigned supreme, giving birth to a society paralyzed by lawlessness. Anarchy was the catalyst that propelled the descent into an abyss of violence and disorder. The once harmonious streets now echoed with the cries of the oppressed and the screams of the lawless.

Anarchy means:

a. governance

b. structure

c. chaos

Cavalcade

With a thunderous roar, a cavalcade of motorcycles roared through the sleepy town, their engines shaking the ground beneath their wheels. The riders, clad in leather, formed a formidable parade that commanded attention at every turn. People lined the streets, their eyes fixated on the spectacle that unfolded before them.

Cavalcade means:

a. procession   b. separate   c. scatter

Devoured

They sank their teeth into the succulent fruits, savoring the burst of flavors that erupted in their mouths. The hungry guests devoured the delectable spread, their plates quickly emptied, their hunger appeased. The feast left an indelible memory, etched in their minds and hearts, as a moment of culinary bliss.

Devoured means:

a. abstain   b. consume   c. reject

Extradite

The notorious criminal, wanted for a string of heinous crimes, finally faced justice as the authorities managed to secure his arrest. The government swiftly moved to extradite him back to his home country, where he would stand trial for his atrocities. The process of extradition involved intricate legal procedures and diplomatic negotiations.

Extradite means:

a. surrender   b. retain   c. protect

Inclination

From a young age, she displayed a natural disposition for music, effortlessly mastering multiple instruments and captivating audiences with her mesmerizing performances. Her talent and passion fueled her dedication, propelling her towards a promising career in the world of classical music. Her inclination towards the harmonies and melodies seemed almost destined.

Inclination means:

a. tendency   b. aversion   c. reluctance

Magnate

As a shrewd and determined entrepreneur, he skillfully navigated the intricate web of business transactions and negotiations, amassing a vast empire and establishing himself as a formidable magnate in the corporate world. His keen instincts and strategic decisions propelled his company to unparalleled success, with his influence reaching far and wide.

Magnate means:

a. pauper   b. tycoon   c. beggar

Palliative

The hospice provided compassionate care, offering curative treatment and support to terminally ill patients. The dedicated team of healthcare professionals aimed to alleviate the pain and suffering of their patients, while also addressing the emotional and psychological aspects of their condition. The palliative measures offered solace and comfort in the face of imminent loss.

Palliative means:

a. soothing   b. aggravating   c. intensifying

Presentiment

A vague sense of unease lingered in the air as she embarked on a journey, a foreboding premonition tugging at the corners of her consciousness. Despite the lack of concrete evidence, the ominous feeling persisted, urging her to proceed with caution. Little did she know that her presentiment would soon be validated by a series of unexpected events.

Presentiment means:

a. assurance   b. intuition   c. certainty

Scapegoat

In the wake of a major corporate scandal, the company desperately sought a scapegoat to deflect public outrage and salvage their reputation. The blame fell upon a dedicated employee, unfairly burdened with the responsibility for the misconduct of others. He was sacrificed to appease the angry masses and restore a semblance of trust.

Scapegoat means:

a. patsy   b. hero   c. savior

Underscore

Throughout literature, the power of symbolism is often utilized to accentuate deeper meaning and themes within a narrative. Through carefully chosen metaphors and recurring motifs, authors employ this literary technique to emphasize significant aspects of their stories. The ability to underscore hidden layers of symbolism adds depth and richness to the reading experience.

Underscore means:

a. emphasize   b. minimize   c. overlook

Anecdote

Woven into the fabric of human conversation, stories serve as captivating and relatable narratives that enhance the exchange of ideas. Whether shared during a casual gathering or presented as illustrative examples, anecdotes carry the weight of personal experiences and can shed light on broader social phenomena. These captivating accounts engage listeners and provide memorable insights.

Anecdote means:

a. tale   b. fact   c. evidence

Celerity

In the fast-paced world of emergency medicine, the ability to respond with celerity is crucial. Doctors and paramedics must swiftly assess the situation, make split-second decisions, and administer life-saving treatments. Every passing moment can make a difference between life and death, underscoring the importance of speed and efficiency in healthcare.

Celerity means:

a. tardiness   b. sluggishness   c. swiftness

Dexterous

The masterful pianist effortlessly commanded the ivory keys, displaying a dexterous flair that astounded the audience. Her fingers danced across the keyboard, executing intricate melodies with precision and grace. The dexterity demonstrated in her performance evoked a sense of awe and admiration from all who witnessed it.

Dexterous means:

a. skillful   b. clumsy   c. awkward

Extraneous

When crafting a concise and coherent essay, it is vital to eliminate any extraneous information that does not contribute to the main argument. Every word and sentence should serve a purpose and support the central thesis. By removing unrelated tangents, the writer can maintain clarity and focus, ensuring a more impactful and persuasive composition.

Extraneous means:

a. irrelevant   b. relevant   c. pertinent

Incoherent

The babble of voices merged into a cacophony of unarticulate sounds, making it difficult to discern individual conversations. The lack of clarity and order dampened the atmosphere, hindering effective communication and understanding. The incoherent chatter highlighted the need for a more organized and structured approach to dialogue.

Incoherent means:

a. articulate   b. logical   c. confused

Maladroit

In the delicate art of culinary mastery, one misstep can alter the entire outcome of a chef's creation. The precision required to combine flavors and execute intricate techniques demands a maladroit touch. As the aspiring chef anxiously presented his dish to the judges, his lack of finesse became unequivocally evident, resulting in a disappointing culinary experience for all.

Maladroit means:

a. skilled   b. adept   c. clumsy

Pallid

The pale moon cast an ethereal glow over the desolate landscape, rendering everything in a pallid hue. The absence of vibrant colors accentuated the melancholic ambiance, evoking a profound sense of serenity tinged with sorrow. The landscape mirrored the state of the protagonist's weary soul.

Pallid means:

a. flushed   b. rosy   c. wan

Presumptuous

With unwavering confidence, the young politician made sweeping assertions without sufficient evidence, displaying a presumptuous disregard for opposing viewpoints. His self-assured demeanor belied a lack of nuance and respect for the complexities of governance. The overconfident nature of his claims left the audience questioning his expertise and judgment.

Presumptuous means:
a. arrogant   b. humble   c. cautious

Scrupulous

Throughout scientific research, the very attention to detail and methodological rigor are paramount. Researchers meticulously design experiments, collect data, and analyze results, leaving no room for error or bias. Through scrupulous adherence to scientific principles, groundbreaking discoveries are made.

Scrupulous means:
a. sloppy   b. meticulous   c. careless

Unequivocal

The judge delivered an unquestionable verdict, leaving no room for doubt or ambiguity. The evidence presented during the trial was incontrovertible, pointing to the defendant's guilt beyond a shadow of a doubt. The resolute and unwavering tone of the judge's voice underscored the unequivocal nature of his statement.

Unequivocal means:
a. clear   b. vague   c. questionable

Animosity

Deep-rooted animosity simmered beneath the surface of the rival clans, passed down through generations like an indomitable flame. The bitter history of conflict and resentment fueled an unyielding hostility that permeated every interaction. The animosity between the two clans reached its climax in a battle that would forever alter their destinies.

Animosity means:
a. hostility   b. amity   c. friendship

Censorious

In artistic expression exists a dichotomy between the desire for creative freedom and the presence of judgmental individuals seeking to stifle innovation. These critical voices ruthlessly dissect every brushstroke and analyze every written word, imposing limitations on the artist's vision. Despite the oppressive atmosphere, the artist bravely perseveres, refusing to succumb to the censorious nature of the art world.

Censorious means:

a. critical   b. approving   c. open-minded

Dichotomy

The social fabric of society is often shaped by a fundamental dichotomy between tradition and progress. While some cling to time-honored customs, others embrace change and innovation. This inherent divide generates intellectual discourse and fuels the evolution of civilizations, constantly navigating the delicate balance between the past and the future.

Dichotomy means:

a. division   b. unity   c. convergence

Extrapolate

In the world of scientific inquiry, researchers often deduce conclusions from a limited pool of data. Through careful analysis and logical deduction, they extend their findings to shed light on broader phenomena. The ability to extrapolate meaningful insights from the smallest sample sizes is a testament to the power of scientific ingenuity.

Extrapolate means:

a. infer   b. confine   c. restrict

Incongruous

The fusion of architectural styles in the cityscape presented an incongruous scene, where sleek modernist structures stood juxtaposed against ornate historical buildings. The clash of aesthetics evoked a sense of bewilderment and provoked contemplation on the passage of time and the evolution of design. The discrepant blend of old and new captivated the onlookers' gaze.

Incongruous means:

a. incompatible   b. harmonious   c. consistent

Malady

Throughout the bustling corridors of the hospital, patients anxiously awaited their turn, each afflicted by a different malady. From common ailments to rare diseases, the diverse range of conditions reminded everyone of the fragility of human existence. The doctors and nurses diligently worked to decipher the root cause of each malady, offering hope and solace to the suffering.

Malady means:

a. vigor   b. wellness   c. illness

Palpable

As tension filled the air, the spectators sensed a perceptible energy, as if the outcome of the match rested on a knife's edge. Every cheer and gasp resonated through the crowd, creating an atmosphere charged with anticipation. When the winning goal was scored, jubilation erupted, and the palpable thrill enveloped everyone in its embrace.

Palpable means:

a. tangible   b. indiscernible   c. invisible

Pretentious

In the high society exists an ever-present desire to appear affluent and cultured, oftentimes leading to pretentious behavior. Individuals adorn themselves with extravagant accessories and pepper their speech with esoteric references in a bid to project an air of superiority. However, beneath their veneer of grandeur, their flaunty nature unravels, revealing their insecurities and lack of authenticity.

Pretentious means:

a. ostentatious   b. humble   c. genuine

Scrutinize

As the case unfolded in the courtroom, the astute lawyers meticulously scrutinized every piece of evidence presented, leaving no stone unturned in their quest for the truth. They examined each witness's testimony with a discerning eye, searching for inconsistencies or hidden motives. It was through their unwavering scrutiny that the veil of deception began to lift, revealing the hidden truths concealed within the complex web of lies.

Scrutinize means:

a. examine   b. overlook   c. ignore

Unfetter

In the pursuit of personal growth, one must have the courage to unfetter themselves from the shackles of self-doubt and societal expectations. The journey towards self-discovery necessitates breaking free from the constraints that stifle individual potential. Only by shedding the burdens of conformity can one embrace their true passions and forge their own path towards fulfillment.

Unfetter means:

a. confine   b. liberate   c. bind

Annex

The history of empires is replete with tales of ambitious rulers seeking to seize new territories, expanding their dominion and influence. Through calculated strategies and military might, they brought smaller regions under their control, subjugating local populations to their rule. The decision to annex neighboring lands was often met with resistance and conflict, as the amalgamation of cultures and power dynamics shifted.

Annex means:

a. divide   b. disassociate   c. acquire

Censure

Public figures often walk a tightrope, constantly aware of the potential for censure from their constituents and opponents. Any misstep or controversial statement can lead to swift condemnation and public backlash. The scrutiny of the media and the public's demand for accountability keep politicians on their toes, ensuring their actions align with the expectations of their constituents.

Censure means:

a. criticize   b. praise   c. commend

Didactic

In our long history, literature has served as an informative tool, aiming to educate and enlighten readers about various aspects of life and human nature. Authors employ narrative and metaphor to convey moral lessons and impart knowledge, subtly encouraging readers to reflect on their own experiences. The didactic nature of literature provides a powerful medium for examining complex themes and fostering personal growth.

Didactic means:

a. entertaining   b. instructive   c. fictional

Extrinsic

Amid human motivation, psychologists often distinguish between intrinsic and extrinsic factors. While intrinsic motivation arises from one's personal interest and satisfaction in an activity, extrinsic motivation stems from extrinsic rewards or pressures. Although rewards like money or recognition may temporarily increase engagement, studies have shown that the intrinsic value derived from personal enjoyment and fulfillment is more enduring and meaningful.

Extrinsic means:

a. outside   b. internal   c. inherent

Inconsequential

In the grand tapestry of existence, countless events unfold, some of great significance, while others are unimportant in the larger scheme of things. These moments may pass by unnoticed, leaving no lasting impact or without any discernible consequence. It is through the lens of hindsight that we realize the value of even the most seemingly inconsequential experiences, as they shape our understanding and contribute to the mosaic of our lives.

Inconsequential means:

a. trivial   b. crucial   c. significant

Malediction

Legends and folklore are often abound with tales of torments and hex, where individuals are believed to possess the power to invoke misfortune upon others through supernatural means. These are imbued with ancient rituals and enigmatic incantations, invoking forces beyond mortal comprehension. Whether these maledictions hold any real power or exist as mere superstition, they continue to fascinate and captivate the human imagination.

Malediction means:

a. curse   b. blessing   c. favor

Panacea

Throughout history, humankind has been in search of the elusive panacea, a solution that can cure all ailments or problems. From ancient herbal potions to modern medical advancements, the pursuit of a universal panacea has been ingrained in our collective consciousness. While no true cure may exist, the quest for knowledge and innovation continue to bring us closer to understanding and alleviating the myriad afflictions that plague humanity.

Panacea means:

a. ailment   b. remedy   c. issue

Prevaricate

In politics and public discourse, it is not uncommon for individuals to intentionally mislead through evasive and ambiguous language. Political figures may employ evasiveness as a strategy to avoid accountability or to manipulate public opinion. However, the consequences of prevarication are far-reaching, eroding public trust and impeding the pursuit of truth and transparency in democratic societies.

Prevaricate means:

a. deceive   b. honest   c. direct

Scuttle

Under the cover of darkness, the tiny creatures of the forest scuttle about, their tiny claws scratching against the forest floor as they seek safety and sustenance. From insects to small mammals, the act of scuttling serves as an essential survival mechanism, allowing them to navigate their environment with agility and stealth. These sounds fade into the background, a hidden symphony only discernible to those attuned to the secrets of the wilderness.

Scuttle means:

a. walk   b. saunter   c. scamper

Unfrock

The village was abuzz with anticipation as the renowned Bishop arrived for his annual visit. His imposing presence demanded respect from the locals who revered him for his vital role in the community. However, on this particular occasion, the villagers were taken aback by his diffident demeanor and the inconspicuous absence of his ecclesiastical garments. Unbeknownst to them, the Bishop had made a fallacious decision that ultimately led to his unfrocking – a consequence that stripped him of his sacred authority and left him in a state of disgrace.

Unfrock means:

a. sanction   b. defrock   c. crown

Vital

It is undeniable that vaccinations play a critical role in preventing the spread of infectious diseases. The impact of immunization extends far beyond individuals, protecting the broader community from potential outbreaks and ensuring public health. Without this vital intervention, vulnerable populations, such as the elderly and the immunocompromised, would be at an increased risk of contracting and succumbing to preventable illnesses.

Vital means:

a. essential   b. optional   c. insignificant

Cerebral

Aspiring scientists immerse themselves in the rational pursuit of knowledge, fueled by an insatiable curiosity about the mysteries of the universe. This journey often involves the exploration of intricate theories, the analysis of complex data, and the application of advanced mathematical concepts. By engaging in such cerebral endeavors, these scholars push the boundaries of human understanding and contribute to the collective wisdom of humanity.

Cerebral means:

a. intellectual   b. instinctive   c. physical

Diffident

The timid student stood before the class, diffidently fidgeting with the edge of his notebook. Despite possessing a brilliant mind and unmatched potential, his diffidence acted as a barrier to his academic success. Overwhelmed by self-doubt and the fear of judgment, he hesitated to voice his ideas, unknowingly depriving his peers and teachers of valuable insights that would have enriched their discussions.

Diffident means:

a. shy   b. bold   c. confident

Fallacious

Fallacious arguments in politics often permeate the rhetoric employed by politicians to sway public opinion. These misleading tactics manipulate emotions and misrepresent facts, serving as a disservice to informed and rational decision-making. By engaging in such reasoning, politicians jeopardize the integrity of the democratic process, hindering the pursuit of truth and compromising the public's trust.

Fallacious means:

a. valid   b. false   c. reliable

Inconspicuous

Amidst the magnificent architecture of the city, nestled within the bustling streets, stood an inconspicuous café. With its unassuming exterior and understated signage, it often went unnoticed by passersby. However, those who ventured inside discovered a hidden gem: a cozy haven where delectable pastries, rich aromas, and warm smiles blended seamlessly, creating an environment that offered respite from the chaos of urban life.

Inconspicuous means:

a. obvious   b. prominent   c. hidden

Malefactor

Throughout history, there have been infamous figures whose names are forever associated with their malevolent deeds. These felons, driven by greed, power, or twisted ideologies, wreaked havoc upon society, leaving behind a trail of suffering and destruction. Despite their egregious actions, it is through the pursuit of justice and moral rectitude that societies strive to apprehend and bring these malefactors to a rightful reckoning.

Malefactor means:

a. wrongdoer
b. innocent
c. virtuous

Paradigm

Scientific discoveries have often led to paradigm shifts, challenging long-held beliefs and expanding our understanding of the natural world. Such upheavals in scientific thought result from the accumulation of evidence that deviates from accepted norms, prompting researchers to reevaluate prevailing paradigms. As new theories emerge, old assumptions are discarded, paving the way for revolutionary advancements in knowledge.

Paradigm means:

a. anomaly
b. model
c. exception

Pristine

Deep within the heart of the Amazon rainforest lies an untouched sanctuary, where nature's beauty remains pristine and untainted by human interference. Towering trees stretch toward the heavens, their branches teeming with vibrant life, while crystal-clear streams cascade through the verdant landscape. Within this pure refuge, biodiversity flourishes, offering a glimpse into a pristine world that remains largely unexplored.

Pristine means:

a. polluted
b. immaculate
c. defiled

Seminary

Nestled amidst rolling hills, the venerable seminary stands as a haven for those seeking a higher calling in religious studies. Here, aspiring clergy immerse themselves in a rigorous academic curriculum, delving into theology, philosophy, and scripture. With the guidance of esteemed scholars and spiritual mentors, these students embrace their vocation, preparing to serve their respective faith communities with unwavering devotion.

Seminary means:

a. theological school
b. secular institution
c. nonreligious school

Unprecedented

The year 2020 unfolded with a global pandemic that brought nations to a grinding halt, initiating an extraordinary crisis that tested humanity's strength and resilience. As the virus spread with alarming speed, governments implemented stringent measures, economies faltered, and millions locked themselves inside their homes. The world watched in awe and trepidation as mankind grappled with an unprecedented challenge, desperately seeking solutions to stem the tide of uncertainty.

Unprecedented means:

a. unparalleled   b. ordinary   c. familiar

Anomaly

In the vast cosmos, astronomers occasionally stumble upon celestial objects that defy conventional explanations. These anomalies, characterized by peculiar behaviors or unexpected properties, captivate the scientific community, sparking fervent investigations and theories. Whether it be an enigmatic star formation or a mysterious cosmic event, anomalies serve as reminders that the universe, in its infinite complexity, still holds many secrets waiting to be unraveled.

Anomaly means:

a. deviation   b. norm   c. conformity

Certitude

The search for certitude has eluded scholars for centuries. Despite fervent debates and rigorous analyses, the question of absolute truth remains a paradoxical enigma, evading definitive resolution. While individuals may find solace in personal convictions, the realm of knowledge demands continuous questioning, recognizing the ephemeral nature of certitude itself.

Certitude means:

a. conviction   b. doubt   c. ambiguity

Digress

During intellectual discussions and oral examinations, students are often cautioned against the temptation to depart from the main topic. To remain focused and cohesive in their arguments, they must resist the tantalizing allure of tangential narratives or irrelevant anecdotes. A disciplined mind can navigate through the vast expanse of knowledge without allowing itself to digress into uncharted territories.

Digress means:

a. adhere   b. conform   c. deviate

Falter

In moments of adversity and uncertainty, even the stoutest of hearts may stumble, confidence shaken by doubt and fear. The path to success is often paved with obstacles, demanding unwavering determination and resilience in the face of setbacks. It is through persistence and an indomitable spirit that one can overcome the challenges that cause others to falter and emerge stronger than ever before.

Falter means:

a. hesitate   b. endure   c. persevere

Indelible

Some artistic creations possess a transformative power, leaving a persistent mark on the collective consciousness of humanity. These masterpieces, be they captivating paintings or poignant literary works, have the ability to transcend time and cultural barriers, evoking a myriad of emotions within their viewers or readers. The impact of such indelible expressions of human creativity endures for generations to come.

Indelible means:

a. erasable   b. permanent   c. fading

Malinger

There are those in academia who seek to evade the rigors of scholarship by employing various stratagems to malinger their true capabilities. Though initially successful in deceiving others, the act of malingering ultimately undermines their own growth and intellectual development. To truly excel and contribute meaningfully to their chosen field, individuals must embrace a mindset of dedication and honest effort.

Malinger means:

a. excel   b. endeavor   c. pretend

Paradox

Within the intricate tapestry of human existence, paradoxes abound, challenging our notions of logic and coherence. Often characterized by seemingly contradictory elements, these puzzles offer fertile ground for intellectual exploration and deep contemplation. By unraveling the enigmatic threads woven within paradoxical statements, we gain new insights that expand our understanding of the world in all its complex nuances.

Paradox means:

a. contradiction   b. certainty   c. clarity

Proclivity

Within the depths of the human mind, there exists a natural tendency towards certain behaviors or interests. These innate tendencies, intricately woven into the fabric of one's being, shape the trajectory of one's life and influence their choices. Whether it be a proclivity towards artistic pursuits, scientific endeavors, or intellectual curiosity, these guide individuals towards the realization of their true passions.

Proclivity means:

a. inclination   b. aversion   c. reluctance

Sensuous

The great Masters of Art have long sought to capture the essence of sensuous beauty, arousing a depth of emotions within the beholder. Through the deft strokes of a paintbrush or carefully chosen words, they evoke a sensory experience that transcends the confines of mere visual or auditory perception. The interplay of color, texture, and form ignites a symphony of sensations, leaving a lasting impression on the viewer's soul.

Sensuous means:

a. bland   b. sensual   c. austere

Unscathed

In the crucible of life, where adversity and challenges abound, there are those who emerge unscathed, their spirits unbroken by the tempestuous winds that threaten to consume them. With unwavering resilience and a steadfast determination, they navigate the treacherous waters, emerging from trials and tribulations with renewed strength and wisdom. Though scarred by the journey, they wear their wounds as badges of honor, testaments to their indomitable spirit.

Unscathed means:

a. unharmed   b. injured   c. harmed

Antagonism

In the complex tapestry of human relationships, the undercurrent of enmity can often simmer beneath the surface, threatening to rupture the fragile harmony that binds individuals together. Whether born out of ideological differences, personal conflicts, or a clash of interests, antagonism breeds discord, hindering collaboration and understanding. It is through empathy and the recognition of shared humanity that we can transcend these barriers and forge a more harmonious coexistence.

Antagonism means:

a. friendship   b. harmony   c. hostility

Charlatan

Amid intellectual discourse, there are those who masquerade as experts, wielding shallow knowledge and deceptive charisma to deceive the unsuspecting. These charlatans, with their silver tongues and dubious claims, exploit the trust of others for personal gain and recognition. However, their facade crumbles under scrutiny, revealing their true nature and exposing their deceit to the discerning eye.

Charlatan means:

a. impostor   b. expert   c. genuine

Dike

In the battle against the relentless forces of nature, humans have developed innovative methods to safeguard their communities, such as the construction of robust dikes. These massive barriers stand as a testament to human ingenuity and engineering prowess, protecting fertile lands and bustling towns from the destructive forces of flooding. The resilience of these dikes, fortified by unwavering determination, ensures that communities remain secure and unyielding in the face of nature's fury.

Dike means:

a. breach   b. opening   c. levee

Fanatical

Amidst human ideologies exist individuals whose unwavering devotion and fervor are unmatched. They become fanatical disciples, possessed by an intense passion and relentless pursuit of their chosen cause. Driven by an unyielding belief, they traverse the borders of reason, sacrificing personal relationships and societal norms in their quest to uphold and propagate their ideals.

Fanatical means:

a. overzealous   b. indifferent   c. apathetic

Indifferent

Studying the complexities of human emotions, there are those who exist in a state of emotional detachment and indifference. They navigate life's challenges with an impartial lens, unswayed by the highs and lows of the human experience. This apparent indifference, though perceived as a lack of empathy, can often be an armor shielding the individual from the overwhelming clamor of emotions in a chaotic world.

Indifferent means:

a. unconcerned   b. caring   c. passionate

Malingerer

In our society, some individuals feign illness or injury to avoid their responsibilities, earning themselves the title of a malingerer. By pretending to be debilitated, they seek to gain sympathy or shirk their duties, undermining the integrity of systems designed to promote productivity and growth. Unmasking the charade, those around them see through their deceit, for the truth will always unveil itself.

Malingerer means:

a. slacker   b. hard-worker   c. diligent

Paragon

There are sometime extraordinary individuals who surpass expectations, embodying the quintessence of excellence. They become paragons of virtue, displaying exceptional talent, wisdom, and integrity in their spheres of influence. Their accomplishments serve as beacons of inspiration, illuminating paths to greatness for those who yearn to follow in their footsteps.

Paragon means:

a. epitome   b. failure   c. average

Procrastinate

In the intricate dance between time and productivity, some of us succumb to the allure of procrastination. Delaying essential tasks and decisions, we surrender to the temptations of momentary satisfaction, disregarding the consequences that loom over our heads like a threatening storm. Breaking free from the shackles of slowness requires a potent combination of self-discipline, motivation, and a steadfast determination to seize the moment.

Procrastinate means:

a. delay   b. expedite   c. prioritize

Sentinel

Standing tall and vigilant, the sentinel embodies unwavering dedication to his assigned task of protection and vigilance. Whether it be the guardians of a castle, a watchful soldier, or a watchman of the night, the duty requires an acute sense of awareness and an unrelenting focus on the preservation of safety. With watchful eyes scanning the horizon, he remain steadfast until the threat is detected and their purpose fulfilled.

Sentinel means:

a. defenseless   b. exposed   c. guard

Unwitting

In espionage, where secrets are concealed beneath veils of deception, there are unsuspecting individuals who unknowingly play a role in intricate plots. These unwitting players become pawns in a larger scheme, their innocence manipulated and exploited for ulterior motives. Oblivious to their unwitting involvement, they only discover the truth when the curtains of deceit are finally lifted.

Unwitting means:

a. aware   b. conscious   c. ignorant

Antagonistic

In human relationships, there exist individuals whose inherent nature is predisposed towards hostility and conflict. Their antagonistic demeanor permeates their interactions, fueling discord and animosity. Unyielding and confrontational, they fan the flames of disagreement, sowing seeds of division wherever they tread.

Antagonistic means:

a. hostile   b. friendly   c. cooperative

Chary

Upon encountering unfamiliar territories or circumstances, precaution prevails in the hearts of the wise. They approach new challenges with a measured and chary disposition, carefully weighing the potential risks and rewards. With guarded steps, they navigate the unknown, mindful of the treacherous paths that may lie ahead.

Chary means:

a. cautious   b. reckless   c. bold

Dilatory

In the ever-flowing river of time, some possess a propensity for delay and procrastination. Their dilatory tendencies hinder progress and productivity, as tasks are perpetually postponed and deadlines inch closer with each passing moment. The weight of unfinished responsibilities makes their shoulders sag, yet they continue to embrace the slow allure, until the impending pressure becomes too great to bear.

Dilatory means:

a. procrastinating   b. prompt   c. punctual

Fanaticism

Throughout human history, some periods are marked by fervent devotion to ideologies, spawning fanaticism that eclipses reason and fuels insurmountable divisions. Fanaticism consumes the minds and hearts of its adherents, blinding them to alternative perspectives and driving them to extreme measures in defense of their belief systems. Only with time and introspection can the flames of fanaticism be quelled, allowing for understanding and reconciliation to take root.

Fanaticism means:

a. tolerance   b. extremism   c. moderation

Indigenous

Living in a mosaic of diverse cultures and societies, indigenous communities have a profound connection to their ancestral lands. They embody the rich tapestry of traditions, customs, and languages that have been passed down through generations. Immersed in the rhythms of nature, they treasure and protect their unique heritage, ensuring its endurance for the generations yet to come.

Indigenous means:

a. foreign   b. imported   c. native

Malleable

The sculptor, like an artist, wields immense power over his malleable medium, effortlessly transforming rigid material into works of breathtaking beauty. His skilled hands shape and mold the clay, bending it to his will and breathing life into their vision. Through his artistry, the sculptor unveils a masterpiece, a manifestation of his creative prowess and the triumph of the malleable nature of their chosen medium.

Malleable means:

a. pliable   b. rigid   c. unyielding

Paramount

In the vast cosmos that stretches beyond the bounds of our vision, stars and galaxies twinkle in a symphony of celestial wonder. Amidst this cosmic grandeur, the gravitational forces that shape the universe play a paramount role. They dictate the dance of celestial bodies, orchestrating the cosmic ballet that dazzles our eyes and ignites our imagination.

Paramount means:

a. predominant   b. minor   c. trivial

Prodigal

Some individuals seduced by opulence and fleeting pleasures, succumb to the allure of prodigality. They squander their fortunes with reckless abandon, living in a gluttonous frenzy that leaves them empty-handed and teetering on the precipice of ruin. Only when they face the stark reality of their prodigal ways do they come to acknowledge the value of prudence and the importance of fiscal responsibility.

Prodigal means:

a. extravagant b. frugal c. prudent

Sequester

In the world of literature, the recluse writer embraces solitude as his faithful companion, sequestering himself from the bustling cacophony of the outside world. Within the confines of his hermitage, he finds respite and inspiration, delving into the recesses of his imagination. It is in this self-imposed situation that he weaves tales that captivate the hearts and minds of readers, his words bridging the gap between fantasy and reality.

Sequester means:

a. expose b. integrate c. isolate

Upbraid

In interpersonal relationships, we witness moments when tensions rise and emotions overflow, leading individuals to upbraid one another. Harsh words are flung like arrows, their aim to wound and strike at the heart of the recipient. Yet amidst the storm of accusations and reprimands, there lies the potential for growth and understanding, as both parties confront their shortcomings and strive for reconciliation.

Upbraid means:

a. scold b. praise c. commend

Antediluvian

In the annals of history, some relics harken back to a time long forgotten, to an antediluvian era lost in the mists of time. These ancient artifacts bear witness to civilizations that flourished and declined, illuminating the path traveled by humanity throughout the eons. As we uncover these remnants of the past, we unveil a tapestry of forgotten wisdom, bridging the gap between the antediluvian world and our present reality.

Antediluvian means:

a. modern b. ancient c. futuristic

Chastises

In the realm of parenting, a wise and caring guardian recognizes the importance of imparting discipline upon the child when necessary. With a gentle yet firm hand, he chastise the youngster for his missteps, steering him towards the path of righteousness and personal growth. Through these corrective actions, parents provide invaluable guidance and nurture their child's development.

Chastises means:
a. praises   b. rewards   c. reprimands

Dilemma

Life's intricate fabric often presents us with perplexing choices, enveloping us in a web of uncertainty and contemplation. Within these constant dilemmas, we find ourselves torn between conflicting desires and values, unsure of the correct path to take. Yet, it is through careful reflection and thoughtful consideration that we navigate the labyrinth of choices and emerge with the clarity needed to make decisive, wise decisions.

Dilemma means:
a. predicament   b. resolution   c. certainty

Fastidious

With impeccable attention to detail and an unwavering commitment to perfection, the fastidious artist brings his creative vision to life. Every stroke of the brush, every note played on the piano, reflects his meticulous nature and unwavering standards. It is through his pursuit of excellence that his creations achieve a level of unrivaled beauty and precision.

Fastidious means:
a. sloppy   b. meticulous   c. careless

Indolence

The lethargy of indolence threatens to engulf individuals, pulling them into a state of idle complacency. With inertia lies the danger of lost opportunities and wasted potential. Only through the recognition of this malaise and the subsequent awakening of motivation can one rise from the clutches of indolence and embark on a path of productivity and personal growth.

Indolence means:
a. inertia   b. diligence   c. productivity

Mallet

The skilled carpenter wields his trusty mallet with precision and finesse. The rhythmic sound of it meeting the chisel resonates throughout the workshop as he carves intricate designs into the sturdy wood. With each strike, the mallet becomes an extension of his determination and expertise, shaping the raw materials into a work of art.

Mallet means:

a. soft

b. gentle

c. hammer

Parasite

Nature's delicate balance can sometimes be disrupted by the presence of a parasitic organism, latching onto its host to thrive and propagate. This insidious interloper feeds off the life force of its unsuspecting victim, sapping their strength and vitality. It is only through vigilant measures and effective eradication methods that we can liberate the host from the clutches of the relentless parasite.

Parasite means:

a. symbiont

b. leech

c. mutualist

Prodigious

In the world of classical music, the prodigious young pianist mesmerized audiences with his unparalleled talent and virtuosity. With nimble fingers dancing across the ivory keys, he breathed life into the timeless compositions of the great masters. The musician's extraordinary gift transcended the boundaries of ordinary human capabilities, leaving the audience in awe.

Prodigious means:

a. ordinary

b. extraordinary

c. average

Serendipity

Life's journey often leads us to unexpected encounters and delightful surprises, giving rise to moments of serendipity. As we navigate the twists and turns of fate, chance and fortune intertwine to orchestrate these unplanned blessings. Serendipity guides us towards unanticipated joys and unforeseen opportunities, enriching our lives in ways we could never have imagined.

Serendipity means:

a. intention

b. fortuity

c. purpose

Uproarious

In the bustling comedy club, the laughter of the audience reverberated throughout the room, punctuating the punchlines delivered by the brilliant stand-up comedian. With masterful timing and witty observations, he had the crowd in stitches. The uproarious atmosphere created an unforgettable night of merriment and pure joy.

Uproarious means:

a. hilarious   b. solemn   c. somber

Anthology

In the annals of literature, an anthology serves as a curated collection of literary treasures, offering readers a diverse range of poems, stories, and essays. From the depths of ancient epics to the vibrant voices of contemporary writers, the anthology weaves together a tapestry of literary brilliance. Each carefully selected piece within it paints a vivid portrait of the human experience.

Anthology means:

a. compilation   b. individual   c. singular

Chicanery

Deep down the murky world of politics, chicanery often weaves its deceptive web, manipulating and distorting the truth for personal gain. Behind the scenes, cunning politicians employ deceit and trickery to sway public opinion and manipulate the outcome of important decisions. Only through vigilance and a discerning eye can we uncover the chicanery and strive for a more transparent and just political landscape.

Chicanery means:

a. deceit   b. honesty   c. sincerity

Dilettante

Art attracts a myriad of enthusiasts, ranging from devoted practitioners to mere dilettantes. While the true artist dedicates his life to the relentless pursuit of creative expression, the dilettante dabbles in various endeavors without true commitment. Although the dabbler may possess a fleeting interest in multiple disciplines, his lack of deep knowledge and expertise sets him apart.

Dilettante means:

a. expert   b. specialist   c. amateur

Fatuous

An individual in politics, with foolish and uninformed decisions, sometimes leave the nation puzzled and dismayed. This particular politician, with his lack of insight and intelligence, consistently displayed a fatuous understanding of complex issues. His shallow reasoning and inability to grasp the intricacies of governance ultimately led to disastrous outcomes.

Fatuous means:

a. foolish   b. wise   c. astute

Inductee

Within the prestigious halls of the Music Hall of Fame, the induction ceremony celebrated the achievements of talented musicians who had left an indelible mark on the industry. As the crowd applauded, the latest inductee took the stage, humbled by the recognition bestowed upon them. Their dedication, creativity, and timeless contributions solidified their place among the legends.

Inductee means:

a. veteran   b. entrant   c. outsider

Manipulatable

In today's technologically advanced world, personal data has become a highly sought-after commodity, making individuals vulnerable to manipulation. Advertisers and tech giants exploit this manipulatable nature of user information to tailor content and advertisements to suit their interests. Awareness and vigilance are crucial in protecting oneself from being controlled or influenced for ulterior motives.

Manipulatable means:

a. exploitable   b. resistant   c. unyielding

Parched

Under the relentless sun of the desert, the parched land craved sustenance, its soil cracked and arid. Endless days without rain transformed the once fertile landscape into a barren wasteland. The withered plants and exhausted animals sought respite from the drought, longing for the life-giving raindrops to quench their parched thirst.

Parched means:

a. dry   b. hydrated   c. moist

Profane

In the solemn halls of the sacred temple, worshippers gathered to pay homage and seek solace in their faith. The air was thick with reverence, and the sacred rituals were carried out with the utmost respect. As the ceremony concluded, the devout congregation bowed their heads in silent prayer, refraining from any profane words or actions.

Profane means:

a. sacred   b. sacrilegious   c. holy

Serene

Perched on the mountaintop, immersed in nature's embrace, a breathtaking vista unfolded before the weary traveler. The serene beauty of the landscape, with its tranquil lakes and majestic peaks, stirred a sense of peace within their soul. As the sun gently set on the horizon, casting a golden glow, the traveler found solace and serenity in nature's embrace.

Serene means:

a. chaotic   b. restless   c. calm

Upshot

In the competitive world of sports, years of training and dedication culminate in the final moments of the championship game. The tension was palpable as the clock ticked down, each team giving their all in pursuit of victory. And in a swift and resounding display of skill, the upshot of their relentless efforts was revealed—the triumphant team emerged as the champions.

Upshot means:

a. result   b. beginning   c. prelude

Anthropocentrism

Throughout history, humans have often regarded themselves as the center of the universe, placing their interests above all other living beings. This anthropocentric worldview has influenced our relationship with nature and the way we perceive our role in the world. However, a growing awareness of interconnectedness and the value of all species challenges the tenets of anthropocentrism.

Anthropocentrism means:

a. ecocentrism   b. biocentrism   c. human-centeredness

Chimerical

Imagination knows no bounds, often giving rise to fantastical creatures and worlds that exist only in the depths of our minds. The chimerical beings that populate mythology and folklore evoke a sense of awe and wonder, blurring the lines between reality and fiction. These mythical creatures leave an indelible mark on our collective imagination, reminding us of the power of the human mind.

Chimerical means:

a. realistic   b. imaginary   c. factual

Diligent

Success rarely falls into the lap of the idle; it is the fruit of assiduous effort and unwavering commitment. The diligent students, armed with determination and a hunger for knowledge, embrace the challenges of academia. Through late nights of study and relentless dedication, they harness their potential and achieve their goals, leaving no stone unturned on the path to excellence.

Diligent means:

a. hardworking   b. lazy   c. slothful

Feasible

With innovation, ideas are abundant, but the true test lies in their feasibility. A visionary mind envisions a future where the impossible becomes possible, but feasibility is the bridge between dreams and reality. A thorough analysis of resources, constraints, and potential obstacles determines whether an idea can be translated into a feasible project.

Feasible means:

a. viable   b. unattainable   c. impossible

Indulgent

Amid the hustle and bustle of modern life, individuals often seek solace and self-care through indulgent practices. A quiet evening spent curled up with a good book, treating oneself to a decadent dessert, or embarking on a rejuvenating spa retreat—all serve as indulgent moments that replenish the soul. By embracing these self-indulgent experiences, one finds balance and rejuvenation in the midst of a demanding world.

Indulgent means:

a. pampering   b. restrained   c. strict

Marred

In art, even the most skilled hands are not immune to the occasional flaw. Such was the case for the renowned sculptor as he meticulously carved his masterpiece from a block of pristine marble. However, an unexpected slip of the chisel marred the delicate features of his sculpture, leaving an indelible mark that reminded him of the imperfections inherent in the pursuit of perfection.

Marred means:

a. flawless   b. untouched   c. blemished

Pariah

In the intricate web of social dynamics exists a somber reality—those deemed different or outcast often find themselves ostracized from society's embrace. The appearance of a new student, with unfamiliar customs and a peculiar accent, unsettled the small high school community, turning the unsuspecting individual into an unfortunate pariah in the eyes of their peers.

Pariah means:

a. outcast   b. popular   c. accepted

Profanity

Language possesses the power to shape the very fabric of society, and with it comes a responsibility to choose our words wisely. Yet, within the cacophony of everyday discourse, profanity infiltrates our conversations like a lewd interloper. It is a mark of courtesy and respect to resist the allure of profanity and instead engage in meaningful and eloquent dialogue.

Profanity means:

a. decorum   b. obscenity   c. civility

Serrated

Thinking about culinary arts, the texture of a well-prepared dish can elevate the dining experience to new heights. The serrated edge of a chef's knife gracefully slices through a crusty loaf of bread, imparting a delicate balance of texture and flavor. The precision of the blade ensures each slice is a testament to the artistry of the chef.

Serrated means:

a. jagged   b. smooth   c. straight

Urbane

Amidst the hustle and bustle of the cosmopolitan city, a class of individuals exists with an air of sophistication and refinement. The urbane gentleman, donning a perfectly tailored suit and exuding an effortless charm, navigates the streets with grace and poise. With each interaction, his elegant demeanor leaves a lasting impression on those fortunate enough to cross his path.

Urbane means:

a. rough   b. suave   c. rustic

Antiquated

The relentless march of time spares nothing in its wake, rendering even the most innovative creations vulnerable to obsolescence. The antiquated machinery, once a marvel of engineering, now stands as a relic of a bygone era, overshadowed by the relentless march of progress. Despite its outdated nature, the antiquated equipment serves as a reminder of the ingenuity that paved the way for modern inventions.

Antiquated means:

a. modern   b. outdated   c. current

Choleric

In the vast tapestry of human emotions, anger, like an uncontrollable wildfire, can consume rationality and breed a temperament as fierce as it is unpredictable. The choleric individual, driven by an innate intensity and a propensity for explosive outbursts, struggles to find solace amidst a world that fails to meet their exacting standards. Their zealous disposition often sets them apart from the more composed and serene individuals they encounter.

Choleric means:

a. irascible   b. tranquil   c. placid

Diorama

Walking through the hallowed halls of museums, a glimpse into history awaits the curious onlooker in meticulously crafted dioramas. These three-dimensional representations encapsulate moments frozen in time, transporting the observer to a vivid re-imagining of the past. The diorama, with its meticulous attention to detail, allows the beholder to appreciate the artistry and craftsmanship involved in recreating historical narratives.

Diorama means:

a. reality   b. tableau   c. actuality

Fecund

Nature, in its infinite wisdom, bestows upon certain regions a bountiful fertility that nurtures life in abundance. The fecund landscape, with its lush greenery and blossoming flora, is a testament to the symbiotic relationship between the earth and its inhabitants. It is within these prolific grounds that the circle of life thrives, imbuing every corner with a sense of vitality and growth.

Fecund means:

a. fertile   b. barren   c. sterile

Inebriation

With merriment and indulgence, the temptations of spirits can steer the soul toward a state of blissful surrender. As the night wore on, laughter filled the air and inhibitions dissolved away, rendering the revelers victims of their own inebriation. The careless abandon with which they embraced the world created a temporary respite from the woes of existence.

Inebriation means:

a. intoxication   b. sobriety   c. temperance

Marshal

In moments of chaos and disorder, the firm hand of a capable leader is essential to restore peace and instill a sense of order. The marshal, with unwavering determination and strategic acumen, commands respect and authority, drifting effortlessly through the throngs of turmoil to enforce justice. It is through their unwavering resolve that society finds solace in knowing that order will prevail over anarchy.

Marshal means:

a. follower   b. commander   c. subordinate

Parity

The pursuit of equality, in politics, stands as a beacon of hope for marginalized communities yearning for recognition. The concept of parity, with its inherent aspiration for fairness and balance, seeks to bridge the gaps that drive division and prejudice. It is through a conscious commitment to it that society evolves and mature, thriving on inclusivity and shared progress.

Parity means:

a. disparity   b. imbalance   c. equality

Profound

Amidst the grand tapestry of human existence, there are moments that stir the soul and impart a deep sense of meaning. Such profundity arises when contemplation transcends the superficial and delves into the realms of introspection and wisdom. It is through these intense experiences that individuals garner insight and navigate the complexities of life, emerging with newfound clarity and understanding.

Profound means:

a. deep   b. superficial   c. shallow

Servile

In the annals of history, the role of servitude has long been a contentious one, spanning from feudal serfs to modern-day employees. Such individual, bound by duty and deference, finds himself tethered to the whims and commands of others. A servile mindset, although at times necessary for survival, carries the risk of subjugation and a loss of individual agency.

Servile means:

a. submissive   b. independent   c. assertive

Usurp

Ambition can breed a relentless desire to seize control, often at the expense of others. The usurper, driven by a hunger for dominion, cunningly maneuvers through the corridors of influence, seeking to dislodge the reigning authority and claim the throne as their own. The act of usurpation, though fraught with risk, stands as a testament to the unyielding nature of human determination.

Usurp means:

a. relinquish   b. uphold   c. seize

Apathetic

Within our emotions, apathy stands as a stark contrast to the passions that drive individuals towards action. The spiritless individual, devoid of enthusiasm or concern, remains untouched by the world around them. It is through the absence of emotion that an apathetic soul becomes detached from the joys and sorrows of life, leaving a void that yearns to be filled.

Apathetic means:

a. passionate   b. indifferent   c. concerned

Chronicler

Throughout time, they have woven tales and preserved the collective memory of civilizations gone by. The chronicler, armed with the quill of knowledge and the parchment of remembrance, chronicles the tides of history for posterity. Through his meticulous recordings, he brings to life the deeds and narratives that shaped the course of humanity.

Chronicler means:

a. forgetful   b. unreliable   c. historian

Dirge

In the sorrowful melodies that echo through the chambers of grief, the dirge stands as a somber hymn of mourning. It is a musical lamentation that accompanies the departure of loved ones, offering solace to those left behind. The haunting dirge weaves together sorrow and melancholy, creating an emotional tapestry that captures the essence of loss and reflection.

Dirge means:

a. elegy   b. celebration   c. anthem

Felicitous

It is a rare and treasured occurrence when words and actions align in perfect harmony, creating a bond that brings joy and fulfillment. A meeting of minds and hearts sets the foundation for enduring connections, where understanding and empathy intertwine, transcending the boundaries of mere acquaintance. Through the exchange of felicitous gestures, individuals find solace and validation, forging a path towards mutual growth and happiness.

Felicitous means:

a. inauspicious   b. unlucky   c. happy

Ineffable

At times, the human experience transcends the boundaries of language, leaving us grasping for words to describe the profound emotions that stir within. In these ineffable moments, the weight of meaning becomes too overwhelming for conventional expression, leading to a silent contemplation of the sublime. It is there that we encounter the inexplicable mysteries and wonders of life, offering glimpses into the vastness of the human spirit.

Ineffable means:

a. indescribable   b. expressible   c. articulate

Marsupial

In the diverse Earth's wildlife, the marsupials stand as a unique and captivating group, distinct in their reproductive biology and evolutionary adaptations. With their characteristic pouches, female marsupials provide a nurturing environment for their young, fostering a connection that is both intimate and protective. From the agile kangaroos bounding across the Australian outback to the sleepy koalas perched in eucalyptus trees, they offer a glimpse into the diversity and adaptability of nature's creations.

Marsupial means:

a. pouch-bearing
b. placental
c. non-marsupial

Parochial

A provincial mindset can hinder progress and breed ignorance, confining individuals within the boundaries of narrow-mindedness and limited perspectives. The parochial individual, rooted in traditions and cultural norms, may struggle to grasp the complex interplay of global dynamics and diverse identities. It is through a broader outlook, one that transcends such thinking, that humanity can foster inclusivity, understanding, and collective growth.

Parochial means:

a. open-minded
b. cosmopolitan
c. insular

Profundity

Within our intellectual exploration lies a treasure trove of profound insights and revelations. The pursuit of knowledge and understanding allows individuals to venture beyond the surface, diving into the ocean of wisdom and profundity that exists within every discipline. It is through this relentless quest that scholars unravel the mysteries of the universe, pushing the boundaries of human understanding.

Profundity means:

a. depth
b. shallowness
c. triviality

Skeptical

Diving in critical thinking and inquiry, skepticism acts as a guiding principle, prompting individuals to question assumptions, scrutinize evidence, and evaluate claims with a discerning eye. The skeptical mind, honed through the rigorous analysis of ideas, probes beneath the surface to unravel the truth from falsehood. It is through a healthy dose of dubiety that individuals navigate the sea of information, safeguarding intellectual integrity and fostering a spirit of inquiry.

Skeptical means:

a. gullible
b. doubtful
c. trusting

Utilitarian

Utilitarianism stands as a consequentialist theory that advocates for actions that maximize overall happiness and minimize suffering. Rooted in the belief that the greatest good should be pursued for the greatest number of individuals, utilitarianism often requires individuals to make decisions based on a rational calculation of costs and benefits. By weighing the potential positive outcomes against the potential negative consequences, one can strive for a utilitarian approach to ethical dilemmas.

Utilitarian means:

a. idealistic   b. impractical   c. pragmatic

Apathy

In the tapestry of human emotions, passivity represents a stark lack of passion or concern, leaving individuals numb to the joys and sorrows of life. Apathy seeps into the core of one's being, sapping away the motivation to engage with the world or to confront the challenges that lie ahead. It is through a collective awakening and a rejection of it that humanity can strive for a more compassionate and vibrant existence.

Apathy means:

a. indifference   b. passion   c. enthusiasm

Circuitous

Life, with its twists and turns, often unfolds along a meandering path, filled with unexpected detours and diversions. Rather than following an unswerving and one-dimensional trajectory, the journey of existence takes individuals on a meandering route, testing their resilience and adaptability. It is along these circuitous routes that individuals encounter diverse perspectives, expand their horizons, and gain a deeper appreciation for the complexities of the human experience.

Circuitous means:

a. winding   b. direct   c. linear

Disapprobation

In our society, disapprobation acts as a powerful form of social control, signaling the collective judgment and censure of individuals' actions. Whether explicit or subtle, it can carry significant weight, shaping the moral landscape within which individuals navigate their choices. It is through a keen awareness of societal disapprobation that individuals can strive to align their actions with accepted norms and values.

Disapprobation means:

a. condemnation   b. commendation   c. approval

Fervor

Human history is replete with moments marked by intense fervor, where passion and dedication ignite collective movements and shape the course of nations. It serves as a catalyst for change, compelling individuals to rally behind causes they believe in with unwavering conviction. It is through fervor, the relentless pursuit of goals, that societies can foster progress, resilience, and a commitment to a shared vision.

Fervor means:

a. indifference   b. lethargy   c. zeal

Inept

Let's consider skills and abilities, where ineptitude represents a lack of proficiency or competence, hindering individuals from achieving their desired outcomes. Such individual grapples with challenges and struggles to navigate even the simplest tasks, often encountering frustration and disappointment along the way. It is through a commitment to learning and growth that one can transcend their ineptitude, honing their abilities and unlocking their potential.

Inept means:

a. incompetent   b. adept   c. skilled

Martinet

In the annals of military history, it emerges as a figure commanding strict discipline and unwavering adherence to regulations. Often perceived as stern and uncompromising, the martinet enforces order and precision within the ranks, leaving no room for insubordination. It is through the unwavering commitment to hierarchy and unquestioning obedience that armies are molded into efficient fighting forces.

Martinet means:

a. disciplinarian   b. lenient   c. permissive

Parody

A playful and often humorous form of artistic expression, mockery takes familiar elements of a work and exaggerates or distorts them for comedic effect. Through clever imitation and satire, parodies can illuminate the flaws and idiosyncrasies of the original, offering both entertainment and insightful commentary. Artists can then simultaneously honor and skewer the cultural touchstones that shape our shared narratives.

Parody means:

a. satire   b. earnest   c. serious

Proletarian

Within socioeconomic classes, they represents the working class, whose labor sustains the foundations of society. Often characterized by their lack of ownership over the means of production, proletarians toil in factories and fields, their efforts fueling the machinery of progress. It is through collective action and solidarity that the proletariat seeks to assert its rights and address the disparities inherent in capitalist systems.

Proletarian means:
a. bourgeois   b. elite   c. blue-collar

Skirmish

Through war, skirmishes represent localized and limited engagements, often marked by sudden combats and swift tactical maneuvers. These minor conflicts serve as precursors to larger battles, testing the resolve and strategies of opposing forces. It is through these skirmishes that military leaders assess their adversaries and adapt their plans, ultimately shaping the outcome of the broader campaign.

Skirmish means:
a. clash   b. harmony   c. truce

Utopian

Imagined realms of ideal harmony and perfection, where utopias captivate the human imagination, offering glimpses of societies free from strife and injustice. Utopian visions envision equitable distribution of resources, harmonious coexistence, and a tranquil existence unmarred by human follies. It is through the pursuit of these ideals that societies strive to transcend their present limitations, aiming for a brighter future.

Utopian means:
a. dystopian   b. flawed   c. idealistic

Apocryphal

Nestled within the folkloric tapestry of tales and legends, apocryphal stories weave together elements of truth and fabrication, blurring the lines between fact and fiction. These narratives, while captivating, lack concrete evidence or historical veracity. Through the scrutiny of scholars and the discerning eye of critical analysis one can separate the apocryphal from the authentic, casting light on the mysteries of the past.

Apocryphal means:
a. authentic   b. fictitious   c. factual

Circumlocution

Within rhetoric and discourse, circumlocution finds its place as a verbose and indirect manner of expression. Through the artful dance of carefully chosen words and elaborate constructions, speakers employ them to convey their message with an air of ambiguity or to evade direct confrontation. However, the labyrinthine nature of equivocations can sometimes hinder clarity and leave listeners yearning for conciseness and forthrightness.

Circumlocution means:

a. verbosity

b. directness

c. conciseness

Discern

In the ever-shifting landscape of information, the ability to tell apart truth from falsehood becomes an invaluable skill. Through careful analysis and astute observation, individuals can discern the hidden motives and agendas that permeate society. It is through this discernment that one can navigate the complexities of the world and separate fact from fiction, ultimately empowering oneself with knowledge and understanding.

Discern means:

a. overlook

b. ignore

c. perceive

Fickle

Like a capricious breeze, the nature of human preferences can be unpredictable. People's whims and desires change with the passing of time, leaving brands and trends to rise and fall in popularity. It is through an understanding of this fickleness that marketers and innovators strive to stay ahead of changing tastes, constantly adapting and reinventing to satisfy the ever-evolving desires of consumers.

Fickle means:

a. changeable

b. steadfast

c. unwavering

Inertia

In physics, inertia manifests as the resistance an object presents to changes in its state of motion. Objects at rest tend to remain at rest, while objects in motion exhibit a resistance to being brought to a halt. This principle extends beyond the realm of physics as a metaphor for human behavior, wherein individuals may be resistant to change or reluctant to take action. Through the recognition of inertia one can employ strategies to overcome obstacles and propel oneself forward.

Inertia means:

a. inactivity

b. motion

c. drive

Masochist

Deep within the recesses of human psychology lie those who derive pleasure from pain and suffering: the masochists. These individuals find gratification in the experience of physical or emotional discomfort, actively seeking out situations that elicit agony. Their exploration of pain can unwrap new depths of sensation, blurring the boundaries of pleasure and anguish.

Masochist means:

a. self-flagellant   c. sadist   c. pleasure-seeker

Parry

Swordplay, or the art of parrying, emerges as a defensive maneuver to deflect or counter an opponent's attack. Skillful parries require agility, timing, and a profound understanding of one's opponent's intentions. The successful execution of a parry that a swordsman can turn an enemy's aggression against them and seize the advantage in combat.

Parry means:

a. attack   b. deflect   c. strike

Prolific

Few can rival the immense productivity and boundless imagination of a prolific artist. With a ceaseless stream of ideas and a relentless drive to bring him to fruition, the artist's work becomes a testament to his remarkable talent and dedication. By consistently producing exceptional works of art, the prolific artist leaves an indelible mark on the world, inspiring both admiration and awe.

Prolific means:

a. barren   b. productive   c. stagnant

Sluggard

Take the human ambition, where the sluggard finds himself at odds with the fervor and industriousness that propel others towards success. Plagued by a lack of motivation and a penchant for indolence, the sluggard's progress is stymied by their own slothful tendencies. While the world moves forward with relentless energy, he remains stagnant, perpetually delayed by a pervasive sense of idleness.

Sluggard means:

a. lazy   b. diligent   c. proactive

Vacillate

Within the tumultuous waters of decision-making, some individuals find themselves trapped in the quagmire of indecision, endlessly vacillating between choices. Torn between conflicting desires and plagued by uncertainty, they are unable to commit to a clear course of action. It is through decisive resolve and unwavering conviction that one can break free from this cycle and forge ahead with confidence.

Vacillate means:

a. waver   b. decide   c. commit

Appease

In diplomacy and conflict resolution, the art of appeasement emerges as a delicate balancing act, aimed at assuaging the concerns and grievances of opposing parties. Through skillful negotiation and strategic concessions, diplomats seek to foster a climate of peace and harmony. However, the pursuit of appeasement must be tempered with the understanding that excessive concessions can lead to the erosion of one's own position and credibility.

Appease means:

a. provoke   b. pacify   c. enrage

Circumscribe

Societal norms and expectations often circumscribe individuals, dictating the boundaries within which they operate. These constraints can hinder personal growth and limit the realization of one's full potential. Yet, within the confines of these limitations, innovative individuals find ways to push against the boundaries, expanding and redefining what is deemed possible.

Circumscribe means:

a. restrict   b. liberate   c. unravel

Discord

Amidst the harmonious symphony of human interaction, dissension emerges as a dissonant note, disrupting the peaceful equilibrium. Born from disagreements and conflicting perspectives, discords serves as a catalyst for change and growth. It is through their resolution that societies have the opportunity to find common ground and progress towards a unified vision.

Discord means:

a. disagreement   c. harmony   c. concord

Finesse

Within arts and aesthetics, finesse reigns supreme as a hallmark of artistic mastery. It is a delicate dance of precision, grace, and subtlety, executed with meticulous attention to detail. The artist's brush strokes, imbued with finesse, breathe life into the canvas, capturing the essence of their subject in a stunning display of skill and creativity.

Finesse means:

a. skill   b. ineptitude   c. rudeness

Inevitable

Throughout our existence, there are certain forces that remain beyond human influence, leading to the inevitability of certain events. They loom on the horizon, casting an undeniable shadow over life's landscape, unyielding to the whims of mortal beings. No matter how hard one may strive to alter their course, the inevitable unfolds with an unwavering determination, rendering resistance futile.

Inevitable means:

a. avoidable   b. certain   c. preventable

Matriarchy

Matriarchy often emerges in human societies as a social structure where women hold positions of power, influence, and authority. In this paradigm, the revered figures and respected leaders are of the female gender, with their wisdom and guidance shaping the course of communities. Through a matriarchal lens, society is imbued with a unique perspective, one that challenges traditional gender roles and fosters gender equality.

Matriarchy means:

a. male dominance   b. female rule   c. sexism

Parsimonious

In the field of personal finance, thrifty individuals display a commendable ability to exercise restraint and frugality in their expenditure. With an unwavering commitment to resourcefulness, they meticulously navigate the ever-changing landscape of needs and wants. Through their parsimonious habits, they manage to maintain a prudent control over their financial affairs, ensuring a stable and secure future.

Parsimonious means:

a. frugal   b. spendthrift   c. prodigal

Proponents

With such ideas and ideologies, they act as champions, fervently promoting their beliefs and convictions. Armed with persuasive rhetoric and a formidable understanding of their principles, they seek to sway hearts and minds to their cause. As the proponents of their respective ideologies, they forge ahead, undeterred by opposition, in pursuit of a world transformed by their vision.

Proponents means:

a. opponents   b. advocates   c. detractors

Smelt

The process of smelting in metallurgy plays a crucial role in extracting pure metals from their ores. Through the application of heat and chemical reactions, raw materials are transformed, leaving behind impurities as slag. In the final stages, the molten metal is carefully poured into molds, solidifying into shapes that embody the culmination of the smelting process.

Smelt means:

a. melt   b. solidify   c. freeze

Vacuous

Because of intellectual pursuits, a vacuous mind stands as an unfilled vessel, devoid of depth and substance. It is a barren landscape where ideas fail to take root, leaving an echoing void. As a singular individual, lacking in curiosity and intellectual vigor, she drifts aimlessly through life, never seizing the boundless opportunities that await.

Vacuous means:

a. empty   b. intelligent   c. insightful

Apprehensive

In the face of the unknown, apprehension lingers like a shadow, casting doubt and uncertainty on the path ahead. It is a cautious hesitation born from the depths of the human psyche, an instinctual response to potential danger or unfavorable outcomes. Such soul, plagued by worry and unease, timidly treads the line between fear and courage, yearning for reassurance in an unpredictable world.

Apprehensive means:

a. confident   b. assured   c. anxious

Circumspect

In our world brimming with complexities and hidden agendas, it emerges as a shield against hasty judgment and misplaced trust. Circumspection is a wise approach, characterized by careful observation and thoughtful consideration. Such individual, ever vigilant, navigates the labyrinth of relationships and interactions with a discerning eye, safeguarding themselves against potential pitfalls.

Circumspect means:

a. reckless   b. cautious   c. impulsive

Discordancy

Within the symphony of our life, discordancy disrupts the harmonious flow, jarring the senses with out-of-tune notes. It is a cacophony that reverberates through the air, creating an unsettling atmosphere. These voices, clashing and conflicting, fracture the unity that binds us, leaving behind a fragmented melody yearning for resolution.

Discordancy means:

a. harmony   b. dissonance   c. agreement

Fitful

Fitful nights of sleep weave a tapestry of fragmented rest and restless dreams. It is a state of irregular slumber, where tranquility eludes grasp and restlessness fills the void. The off-and-on sleeper, tossed amidst the waves of insomnia, longs for the respite of a peaceful night's rest, a sanctuary in an ever-churning world.

Fitful means:

a. restful   b. peaceful   c. intermittent

Inexorable

Engulf in the intricate web of time and fate, the inexorable march propels us forward, unyielding to pleas and resistance. It is a relentless force, unswayed by human desires or ambitions, sweeping us along its uncharted path. The adamant passage of time, marked by moments of triumph and loss, reminds us of our transient existence, leaving behind a legacy forged among the annals of history.

Inexorable means:

a. flexible   b. relentless   c. changeable

Maverick

With conformity, where societal norms dictate the path one should tread, he emerges as a rebel with a cause. He is an individual who defies convention, charting his own course with audacious confidence and fearless conviction. The maverick, a defiant symbol of individuality and nonconformity, stands apart from the crowd, challenging the status quo.

Maverick means:

a. renegade   b. traditionalist   c. follower

Parsimony

Wandering within the labyrinth of financial choices, the virtue of parsimony shines as a guiding light. It is a quality that fosters frugality and prudent resource allocation, a distinction betwixt wants and true needs. The individuals, disciplined in their fiscal pursuits, astutely navigate the treacherous waters of consumerism, carving a path towards financial stability.

Parsimony means:

a. frugality   b. extravagance   c. prodigy

Prosaic

In a world inundated with endless streams of information, the prosaic man fails to captivate the imagination, lacking in creative depth and lyrical beauty. It is a dullness that permeates the mundane, leaving the senses unstimulated and the mind detached. The uninteresting utterances, void of poetic fervor, wither away in the presence of true literary magnificence.

Prosaic means:

a. poetic   b. mundane   c. imaginative

Smorgasbord

Among the feast of culinary delights, it stands as a tantalizing spread, a cornucopia of flavors and delectable indulgences. Smorgasbord is a sensory overload, where every taste and aroma tantalizes the palate, leaving one yearning for more. There, a culinary symphony, celebrates the diversity of cuisine, uniting cultures through the universal language of food.

Smorgasbord means:

a. buffet   b. scarcity   c. deprivation

Vagrant

In the shadows of bustling city streets, he finds solace amidst the fleeting anonymity of urban life. The vagrant is an individual adrift, transient and detached from the conventional trappings of society. He, a wanderer seeking respite and survival, languishes in the margins of a world that often neglects their plight.

Vagrant means:

a. settled   b. stable   c. homeless

Arable

On nature's canvas, the endless fields stretch as far as the eye can see, a symphony of fertility and agricultural potential. It is a land ripe with opportunity, ready to yield bountiful harvests and sustenance for generations to come. The arable landscape, a testament to the resilience of the earth, beckons farmers to sow the seeds of prosperity.

Arable means:

a. cultivable   b. infertile   c. barren

Circumvent

In politics, where strategies and maneuvers shape the course of power, savvy politicians seek to circumvent the obstacles that obstruct their objectives. It is a skillful dance, an art of navigating through intricate channels to achieve desired outcomes. A politician adept in the art of circumvention employs tactical finesse, avoiding hindrances to achieve their goals.

Circumvent means:

a. bypassing   b. confront   c. tackle

Discrepancy

Precision reigns supreme in data analysis. Any inconsistency is a persistent specter that challenges the validity of findings. It is an incongruity, a divergence between expected and observed values, causing researchers to question the accuracy of their measurements. The discrepancy, a puzzle to be untangled, beckons the inquisitive mind to seek hidden truths.

Discrepancy means:

a. agreement   b. consistency   c. disparity

Flagrant

In sportsmanship, where fair play and ethical conduct are paramount, the foul disrupts the harmony of the game. It is an egregious violation, an act committed with strident disregard for the rules and spirit of competition. The flagrant foul, a stain upon the purity of the match, invites swift retribution and sanctions.

Fragrant means:

a. subtle　　　　　　　b. blatant　　　　　　　c. concealed

Inexpedient

Through the process of decision-making, where consequences weigh heavily upon the path chosen, opting for the inexpedient course can yield disastrous outcomes. It is a foolish choice, one made without prudent foresight or consideration of potential ramifications. The inexpedient decision, fueled by short sightedness, leads down a treacherous path fraught with regret.

Inexpedient means:

a. prudent　　　　　　　b. unwise　　　　　　　c. practical

Meager

Hunger, where sustenance is a scarce commodity, rations offer little reprieve to the famished masses. It is a pittance, an insufficient portion unable to satiate the gnawing emptiness within. The meager provisions, a stark reminder of scarcity, exacerbate the gripping claws of deprivation.

Meager means:

a. scant　　　　　　　b. abundant　　　　　　　c. ample

Partisan

In politics, where conflicting ideologies shape the landscape of discourse, the partisan voter ardently supports his chosen party. It is an allegiance, rooted in unwavering loyalty and steadfast belief in the party's principles. The voter, entrenched in his convictions, vehemently champions his preferred candidate with fervor and enthusiasm.

Partisan means:

a. supporter　　　　　　　b. impartial　　　　　　　c. neutral

Proscribe

In the annals of history, there are instances where societies have deemed certain practices as unworthy and have sought to proscribe them from their midst. It is a declaration of prohibition, a formal denouncement of behavior considered detrimental or morally reprehensible. The edict to veto serves as a stark warning, with transgressors facing severe consequences.

Proscribe means:
a. allow   b. permit   c. forbid

Solace

Through our life's turmoil, when one's spirit is battered by tribulations, solace can be found in the embrace of a loved one. It is a reassuring refuge, a source of consolation and reassurance. The gentle words spoken and the warmth of their presence offer solace, soothing the restless soul.

Solace means:
a. comfort   b. torment   c. agony

Vapid

In literature, words have the power to transport readers to realms unimaginable. An unexciting story fails to ignite the imagination. It is a lackluster narrative, devoid of depth and substance, leaving readers yearning for more. The vapid tale, a mere collection of words without resonance, fails to leave a lasting impression.

Vapid means:
a. insipid   b. engaging   c. stimulating

Arbitrary

Where the decisions of those in power shape the lives of the governed, a discretionary ruling can ignite discontent and breed resentment. It is a decision made without logical reasoning or principled justification, causing confusion and eroding trust. An arbitrary decree, lacking legitimacy, undermines the foundations of a just society.

Arbitrary means:
a. random   b. reasoned   c. justified

Clairvoyant

In the sphere of metaphysics, where the boundaries of the tangible and the unseen intertwine, the clairvoyant possesses the ability to perceive hidden truths and foresee events yet to unfold. It is a gift of heightened perception, a sixth sense that surpasses the limitations of ordinary cognition. His visions, a manifestation of supernatural insight, offer glimpses into the unknown.

Clairvoyant means:

a. unaware   b. oblivious   c. psychic

Discriminate

Equality and fairness are fervently pursued in social justice. To discriminate against a person based on their ethnicity or gender is a grave injustice. It is an act of prejudice, engendered by preconceived notions and unfounded biases. The decision to discriminate, a stark violation of human rights, perpetuates inequality and divisiveness.

Discriminate means:

a. differentiate   b. include   c. embrace

Flamboyant

In the fashion world, where self-expression and creativity converge, the fancy attire of certain individuals serves as a vibrant display of their exuberant personalities. Their ensembles burst with vivid colors and intricate designs, capturing the attention of onlookers. The flamboyant fashionistas, with their audacious style, leave an indelible mark on the runway.

Flamboyant means:

a. ostentatious   b. modest   c. subdued

Infallible

In mathematics, where precision and accuracy reign supreme, a proof is a cornerstone of theorem construction. It is an irrefutable demonstration of logical reasoning and mathematical prowess. The infallible arguments put forth by astute mathematicians stand as testaments to the unyielding laws of numbers.

Infallible means:

a. imperfect   b. unreliable   c. flawless

Meander

In the horizon, the river meander through sprawling landscapes, its bends and curves create intricate patterns that mimic life's winding journey. The waterways, with their leisurely pace, offer moments of tranquility amidst the surrounding chaos. As the river curves gently through the valley, it whispered secrets of ancient tales.

Meander means:

a. wander b. direct c. straighten

Pathos

In the world of theater, where emotions are brought to life on the stage, the portrayal of intense human suffering evokes pathos within the hearts of the audience. It is a poignant display of grief, wrenching at the core of collective empathy. The pathos in the actor's voice resonated deeply, invoking tears in the eyes of spectators.

Pathos means:

a. apathy b. sorrow c. indifference

Prosody

Looking into poetry, where language intertwines with melody, prosody ensures the rhythm and cadence of verse. This art of infusing musicality into words guides the flow of expression. The poet's mastery of it lent a melodious quality to the sonnet, captivating listeners with its enchanting verses.

Prosody means:

a. meter b. dissonance c. incoherence

Solicit

Entrepreneurs in commerce seek to engage customers, and the act of soliciting feedback is essential for business growth. It is the proactive pursuit of opinions and suggestions, fostering a customer-centric approach. The salesperson diligently solicited feedback from patrons, eager to improve their products and services.

Solicit means:

a. request b. discourage c. dissuade

Variegated

In the vibrant gardens of botanical wonder, a variegated tapestry of flowers unfolds, showcasing nature's artistic prowess. Each petal bears a unique hue, blending harmoniously to create an enchanting mosaic of colors. The assorted blooms, with their exquisite patterns, attract pollinators and mesmerize all who behold their beauty.

Variegated means:

a. uniform   b. monotonous   c. diverse

Arcane

Throughout our reading of ancient texts and hidden knowledge, lies the study of esoteric secrets, known only to a select few. These teachings delve into mystical realms, offering tantalizing glimpses into the unknown. The ancient wizard revealed the arcane spell book, its pages filled with cryptic symbols and incantations.

Arcane means:

a. mysterious   b. familiar   c. common

Clamor

Inside the bustling marketplace, a cacophony of voices rises in clamor, as vendors vie for attention. The noisy hubbub echoes through the narrow streets, each merchant fervently calling out their wares. The noise subsided as the king's proclamation resonated with authority.

Clamor means:

a. uproar   b. silence   c. quiet

Discursiveness

Through philosophical debates, intellectuals engage in verbosity, exploring various arguments and counterarguments. Their discussions meander through intricate webs of ideas, seeking to illuminate greater truths. The professor's lecture displayed a remarkable discursiveness, covering a wide array of topics in a single sitting.

Discursiveness means:

a. digression   b. conciseness   c. brevity

Flaunt

Immersed in the fashion world, some individuals choose to exhibit their unique sense of style, using clothing as an expressive medium. They boldly adorn themselves with striking ensembles, reveling in the attention they attract. There, the fashionista confidently flaunt her avant-garde outfit at the gala event.

Flaunt means:

a. hide   b. downplay   c. display

Infamous

In the annals of history, certain figures have gained infamy through their dastardly deeds, forever etching their names in the collective memory. They were fated to be remembered not for their virtue, but for their sinister actions. Some tyrant's reign of terror was infamous throughout the land.

Infamous means:

a. notorious   b. famous   c. honorable

Mellow

As the sun gracefully descended below the horizon, casting a warm glow upon the serene landscape, a mellow atmosphere settled over the countryside. The gentle breeze rustled the leaves, calming the senses and inducing a sense of tranquility. There, the old man sat on the porch, sipping his tea, savoring the mellow flavors that danced upon his palate.

Mellow means:

a. intense   b. energetic   c. relaxed

Patron

The esteemed art gallery attracted a diverse array of customers, each with a discerning eye for exquisite craftsmanship. They perused the halls with a refined taste, examining the brushstrokes and admiring the artistry displayed. One wealthy benefactor, known for his philanthropy, proudly proclaimed himself as a loyal patron of the arts.

Patron means:

a. supporter   b. critic   c. detractor

Prostration

In the solemn temple, devout worshippers bowed in prostration, a symbol of surrendering themselves to a higher power. Their bodies lowered, touching the ground in humble reverence. The prayers were offered with unwavering devotion, seeking solace and enlightenment.

Prostration means:

a. standing   b. submission   c. defiance

Somnambulist

Under the veil of nightfall, a peculiar figure emerged from the shadows, wandering the streets with an otherworldly grace. He, the somnambulist, moved with a dreamlike fluidity, oblivious to the world around, lost in the depths of a subconscious realm. Slowly awakening from his nocturnal trance, he found himself at the edge of a precipice.

Somnambulist means:

a. sleepwalker   b. alert   c. conscious

Vehemence

Passions ignited, words flowed with fiery intensity, as the debate unfolded with fervent vehemence. The speaker's voice reached a crescendo, punctuated by emphatic gestures. The crowd was left in awe, pondering the weight of the speaker's earnest words.

Vehemence means:

a. apathy   b. inertia   c. passion

Archaic

On dusty shelves of the antiquarian bookstore, countless volumes lay filled with archaic knowledge, awaiting the curious minds who sought ancient wisdom. The fragile parchment pages whispered tales of forgotten eras, connecting the present to a bygone time. The scholar unearthed an old manuscript that held the key to deciphering a lost language.

Archaic means:

a. modern   b. outdated   c. current

Clandestine

Deep within the heart of the ancient castle, concealed behind towering walls and secret passageways, a hidden meeting took place under the dim candlelight. Whispers filled the air as conspirators huddled together, their faces masked by shadows, plotting their next move in utmost secrecy. The clandestine affair unfolded, unbeknownst to the watchful eyes of the outside world.

Clandestine means:

a. covert   b. open   c. public

Disdain

With a haughty expression and a subtle curl of the lip, the noblewoman surveyed the room with disdain, dismissing the mere mortals with a flick of her hand. The ostentatious display of wealth and extravagance failed to impress her refined sensibilities. Her dislike for the superficiality of the high society was evident in her every mannerism.

Disdain means:

a. admiration   b. respect   c. contempt

Flippant

In the midst of a serious discussion, his light-minded remarks injected an air of levity, trivializing the weighty matters at hand. His casual attitude and careless demeanor elicited both amusement and irritation from those listening. His flippant response demonstrated a lack of regard for the importance of the subject matter.

Flippant means:

a. frivolous   b. serious   c. thoughtful

Infer

Through careful observation and deductive reasoning, the detective was able to infer the hidden truth behind the cryptic clues. The pieces of the puzzle gradually fell into place, leading him to the undeniable conclusion. With conviction, he confronted the suspect, confident in the evidence he had gathered.

Infer means:

a. guess   b. deduce   c. speculate

Menagerie

The grand theater was transformed into a fantastical menagerie as the circus rolled into town. Acrobats soared through the air, clowns entertained with their jests, and tamed beasts from distant lands gracefully performed tricks. The audience marveled at the sight of the vibrant exhibit before their eyes.

Menagerie means:

a. zoo   b. bareness   c. absence

Patronize

With an air of superiority, the professor patronized his students, belittling their intellectual abilities. His condescending tone and constant interruptions left the room filled with an uncomfortable silence. The students yearned for an environment where their ideas would be validated rather than patronized.

Patronize means:

a. condescend   b. respect   c. honor

Protagonist

As the sun dipped below the horizon, casting an ethereal glow upon the golden wheat fields, the young farmer stood tall, ready to face the challenges that lay ahead. With unwavering determination and an unyielding spirit, he embarked on a journey that would shape not only his destiny but also the lives of those around him. Little did he know that he would soon become the unlikely protagonist of an epic tale of resilience and triumph.

Protagonist means:

a. hero   b. villain   c. antagonist

Soothsayer

In a small village nestled among towering mountains, there lived an enigmatic figure known as the soothsayer. Clad in flowing robes and possessing piercing eyes that seemed to hold the secrets of the universe, she offered glimpses into the realm of the unknown. Villagers sought her counsel, hanging onto her every word, as they yearned for her prophetic wisdom to guide them through life's uncertainties.

Soothsayer means:

a. skeptic   b. realist   c. oracle

Vehement

The courtroom was consumed by the fervor of the defense attorney as he passionately argued for his client's innocence. His words echoed through the hallowed halls, each syllable punctuated by a resounding conviction that left no doubt about his unwavering belief. The jury sat captivated by his vehement defense, swayed by the power and intensity of his argument.

Vehement means:

a. passionate   b. calm   c. indifferent

Archetype

In literature, certain characters embody enduring and universal qualities, becoming archetypes that resonate with audiences across time and cultures. From the tragic hero to the sly trickster, these models serve as a compass guiding readers through the depths of human experience. Through their struggles and triumphs, they illuminate the collective consciousness, offering insights into the complexities of the human condition.

Archetype means:

a. prototype   b. atypical   c. deviation

Clemency

He stood before the judge, his eyes brimming with remorse and regret. Pleading for mercy, he implored the court to show him leniency, to afford him a chance at redemption. As the judge deliberated, the weight of the evidence and the impact of the crime tugged at the scales of justice, ultimately determining whether his plea for clemency would be granted.

Clemency means:

a. mercy   b. harshness   c. punishment

Disinterested

The seasoned art critic approached each masterpiece with an impartial gaze, carefully evaluating artistic technique and composition, unaffected by personal bias. His objective analysis transcended personal preferences, allowing him to offer unbiased insights into the artist's intent. With disinterested expertise, he navigated the myriad of artistic styles, unraveling the underlying narratives woven within each canvas.

Disinterested means:

a. biased   b. invested   c. detached

Flout

In the bustling city streets, amidst the cacophony of horns and the swarm of pedestrians, a rebel emerged. With an air of defiance and a disregard for social conventions, he flouted the norms that restrained others. His audacious actions challenged the status quo, as he fearlessly embraced a life unfettered by conformity.

Flout means:

a. violate   b. adhere   c. conform

Ingénue

Inside the theater, the ingénue graced the stage with her innocence and vulnerability. She captivated audiences with her wide-eyed wonder and soft heartedness, effortlessly evoking empathy with every word she spoke. The young actress breathed life into her character, embodying the essence of youth and naivety.

Ingénue means:

a. innocent   b. experienced   c. worldly

Mendacious

The politician's words dripped with deceit as he weaved a web of falsehoods and half-truths. Every eloquently spoken sentence concealed a hidden agenda, carefully constructed to manipulate public opinion. With a mendacious smile, he deceived the people, betraying their trust for his own gain.

Mendacious means:

a. deceitful   b. truthful   c. candid

Paucity

In the barren desert, where the sun's relentless rays scorched the unforgiving earth, there was a paucity of water. The parched land thirsted for even a drop of moisture, but the arid landscape yielded little respite. The absence of rainfall accentuated the harshness of the environment, forcing inhabitants to endure unrelenting drought.

Paucity means:

a. plenty   b. plethora   c. dearth

Protean

The artist's work was a testament to his protean talents, constantly evolving and defying categorization. His brush danced across the canvas, effortlessly transitioning from vibrant hues to delicate lines. The fluidity of his artistic expression revealed a chameleon-like ability to adapt and transform, leaving viewers in awe of his boundless creativity.

Protean means:

a. unchanging   b. versatile   c. static

Sophomoric

Amidst the hallowed halls of academia, there were those who clung to sophomoric beliefs, refusing to broaden their intellectual horizons. Their puerile antics and shallow perspectives showcased an immaturity that belied their supposed education. The pursuit of higher knowledge was stifled by their superficial engagement with complex ideas.

Sophomoric means:

a. mature   b. juvenile   c. wise

Venal

In the murky world of politics, one must tread carefully to avoid the allure of venal temptations. The promise of power and wealth often leads individuals astray, their moral compass compromised by avarice and corruption. The dishonest nature of their actions betrays the trust of the very citizens they were elected to serve.

Venal means:

a. ethical   b. corrupt   c. virtuous

Archives

Within the dusty corridors of the grand library, the archives held the secrets of civilizations long past. A labyrinth of meticulously cataloged documents, each shelf housed a wealth of knowledge awaiting discovery. Scholars and researchers alike delved into the depths of the collections, unraveling the enigmatic threads of history.

Archives means:

a. records   b. void   c. absence

Cliché

As the sun set on the idyllic beach, a young couple strolled hand in hand, embracing the cliché of a perfect romance. Their love, though genuine, followed the familiar script of whispered promises and stolen kisses. The world around them faded into irrelevance as they fell victim to the timeless allure of the cliché.

Cliché means:

a. original   b. stereotype   c. unique

Disparage

With venomous words dripping from his tongue, he sought to belittle the achievements of others. His envious nature compelled him to denigrate the accomplishments that he himself could not attain. But his attempts to disparage their worth only revealed his own insecurities, leaving him isolated and bitter.

Disparage means:

a. praise   b. admire   c. criticize

Flustered

In the midst of the bustling marketplace, she found herself perturbed and overwhelmed by the cacophony of sounds and the press of bodies. Her mind struggled to keep pace with the rapid transactions and constant demands. But amidst the chaos, she found solace in a deep breath, allowing herself a moment of respite from the flustered frenzy.

Flustered means:

a. agitated   b. unruffled   c. calm

Ingrate

With each act of kindness bestowed upon him, he remained an ingrate, never showing gratitude for the generosity others extended. His selfless gestures went unappreciated, as he took their assistance for granted. The ingratitude he displayed severed the bonds of goodwill, leaving him isolated and devoid of true companionship.

Ingrate means:

a. indebted   b. grateful person   c. moocher

Mercenary

In the ancient time of warriors and conquests, a skilled mercenary traversed the lands, his allegiance easily swayed by the promise of gold. His sword, an extension of his treacherous nature, knew no loyalty but to the highest bidder. With his cunning tactics and ruthless demeanor, he cut a path of chaos and uncertainty, leaving only shattered kingdoms in his wake.

Mercenary means:

a. hired gun   b. devoted   c. altruistic

Peccadillo

Amidst the grand façade of society, the whispers of scandal often centered around a peccadillo, an indiscretion that threatened to tarnish one's reputation. It was the slight misstep, the hidden transgression that held the power to unravel the carefully woven tapestry of one's public persona. In the hushed circles of gossip, the peccadillo held a tantalizing allure, a secret shared among the elite.

Peccadillo means:

a. minor offense   b. virtue   c. integrity

Protégé

Under the tutelage of a skilled leader, the young protégé blossomed into a prodigious talent, his potential shining like a beacon in the realm of their chosen craft. Guided by the wisdom and experience of his teacher, he embarked on a journey of growth and self-discovery. His successes mirrored the dedication and guidance bestowed upon him by his esteemed teacher.

Protégé means:

a. mentor   b. apprentice   c. guide

Soporific

As the sun dipped below the horizon, casting a golden glow over the sleepy town, the soporific embrace of the night settled upon its inhabitants. The gentle rustle of leaves and the soft hum of crickets created a lullaby that beckoned them to surrender to slumber. The tranquility of the night lulled them into a deep and peaceful sleep.

Soporific means:

a. hypnotic   b. stimulating   c. awakening

Veneer

Beneath the flawless veneer of her opulent lifestyle, there lay a sea of carefully concealed insecurities and shattered dreams. The elegant smile and designer garments served as a shield, guarding against prying eyes and superficial judgments. But within the polished exterior, she yearned for authenticity, longing for someone who would see beyond the surface and embrace the flawed beauty within.

Veneer means:

a. façade   b. reality   c. core

Articulate

With each carefully crafted phrase, she painted vivid images in the minds of her audience, her words flowing like a symphony of eloquence and precision. An articulate speaker, she commanded attention with a grace and clarity that left her listeners mesmerized. Her gift for expression surpassed mere communication, transcending language to evoke emotions and provoke thought.

Articulate means:

a. eloquent   b. mumbling   c. silent

Clientele

In the bustling streets of a metropolitan city, a renowned boutique thrived on the patronage of its exclusive clientele. Their discerning taste and appreciation for luxury propelled the boutique to new heights of success. With their unwavering loyalty and refined sensibilities, clients became ambassadors for the brand, spreading its allure far and wide.

Clientele means:

a. customers   b. passersby   c. strangers

Disparity

Within the social fabric of society, a stark disparity existed between the haves and the have-nots, a glaring reflection of the inequalities that plagued the system. While some reveled in opulent splendor, others struggled to meet their basic needs. The chasm of disparity threatened to undermine social cohesion and amplify existing tensions.

Disparity means:

a. inequality   b. parity   c. uniformity

Fly-by-night

A fly-by-night company emerged like a phantom, enticing unsuspecting customers with promises of quick riches and instant success. Unburdened by ethics or long-term commitments, it swooped in and vanished just as swiftly, leaving behind a trail of shattered dreams and broken trust. The fly-by-night operation epitomized the perils of unchecked opportunism.

Fly-by-night means:

a. short-lived   b. established   c. enduring

Inimical

In the heart of the ancient forest, a sense of foreboding hung heavy in the air, as if the very essence of the woods were unfriendly to intruders. The towering trees stood as silent sentinels, their twisted branches and shadowy caverns evoking a primal fear. Nature's wrath lay dormant, but a single misstep could awaken its inimical power.

Inimical means:

a. friendly   b. favorable   c. hostile

Mercurial

Like a tempestuous storm, his emotions fluctuated with intensity, causing ripples of unease and uncertainty among those close to him. One moment he exuded charm and charisma, the next he seethed with rage. His mercurial nature made it impossible to predict his moods or decipher the intricate workings of his mind.

Mercurial means:

a. volatile   b. steady   c. stable

Pedant

Clad in academic robes and armed with a vast array of knowledge, he held court in the hallowed halls of higher education. Every word uttered was meticulously scrutinized, and every grammatical slip met with a swift correction. Despite his encyclopedic wisdom, some viewed this pedant as an obstacle to creativity and a slave to minutiae.

Pedant means:

a. know-it-all   b. novice   c. ignoramus

Protocol

In the grand halls of diplomacy, a meticulously crafted code of conduct guided the interactions between nations. The intricate dance of formalities ensured that every step was executed with precision and decorum. From the exchange of diplomatic gifts to the seating arrangements at high-level summits, protocol governed the delicate balance of international relations.

Protocol means:

a. informality   b. etiquette   c. disregard

Sparse

Amidst the arid landscapes of the desert, life struggled to gain a foothold. The scorching sun and relentless winds sculpted a barren terrain, where water and vegetation were limited. Only the most resilient plants and creatures could survive in the sparsely populated ecosystem, adapted to endure the harsh conditions.

Sparse means:

a. abundant   b. scarce   c. profuse

Venerate

Gathered within the ancient temple, devotees bowed their heads in reverence, honoring their deities with unwavering loyalty. Eyes filled with devotion and hearts burdened with gratitude, they venerated the gods, seeking blessings and guidance. The divine presence enveloped the worshippers, instilling a profound sense of awe and spiritual connection.

Venerate means:

a. worship   b. despise   c. mock

Artifice

On the theatrical stage, an intricate web of manoeuvre unfolded, captivating the audience with its illusionary spell. Behind the scenes, skilled artisans meticulously crafted the elaborate sets and extravagant costumes, creating a world of make-believe. The artifice of the performance transported the spectators into a realm where reality seamlessly blended with imagination.

Artifice means:

a. authenticity   b. sincerity   c. deception

Coalesce

Within the crucible of creativity, disparate ideas and perspectives merged and coalesced, giving birth to a masterpiece. Like molten metals fusing together, the minds of artists and thinkers united to form a symphony of innovation. Boundaries dissolved, and a harmonious whole emerged from the coalescence of individual visions.

Coalesce means:
a. unite   b. divide   c. disperse

Dispassionate

In the sterile confines of the operating room, the surgeon wore a dispassionate mask, allowing clinical judgment to prevail over personal emotions. With steady hands and an analytical mind, they dissected the intricacies of the human body, detached from the narrative of pain and suffering. This approach ensured the highest standards of medical care.

Dispassionate means:
a. impartial   b. biased   c. passionate

Forensic

In the intricate world of criminal investigations, science played a pivotal role in unraveling mysteries and delivering justice. Through meticulous analysis of evidence and careful examination of crime scenes, forensic experts pieced together the puzzle, unveiling hidden truths. Ultimately, it was this evidence that provided the conclusive proof needed to solve the case.

Forensic means:
a. investigating   b. anecdotal   c. speculative

Innate

Deep within the core of every living being resided a natural drive for survival. It was an instinct passed down through generations, encoded in our genetic makeup. This innate sense propelled us forward, enabling us to adapt to our surroundings and overcome adversity, ultimately leading to our flourishing.

Innate means:
a. acquired   b. learned   c. inherent

Merge

In the fast-paced world of business, mergers and acquisitions were a common occurrence. Companies sought to merge their resources, knowledge, and strengths, creating a new entity with greater potential. Through this strategic alliance, they aspired to achieve growth, diversification, and a competitive advantage in the market.

Merge means:

a. separate   b. combine   c. detach

Pedestrian

The bustling city streets were abuzz with a constant stream of activity. People hurried along the sidewalks, lost in their own thoughts, or engaged in animated conversations. Amidst the urban chaos, the pedestrian culture thrived, capturing the essence of a metropolis in perpetual motion.

Pedestrian means:

a. walkers   b. unique   c. extraordinary

Provincial

Nestled in a quiet countryside, with rolling hills and quaint villages, the provincial charm exuded an air of tranquility distinct from the urban landscape. Life moved at a slower pace, grounded in timeless traditions and close-knit communities. This lifestyle offered respite from the chaos of the city, inviting visitors to unwind and reconnect with nature.

Provincial means:

a. rural   b. urban   c. metropolitan

Specious

Beneath the veil of apparent reason, a gilded argument masqueraded as a legitimate perspective. It lured unsuspecting minds with its superficial logic, obfuscating the truth and manipulating perceptions. However, a discerning observer could see through the specious facade, recognizing the fallacies and inconsistencies concealed within.

Specious means:

a. valid   b. genuine   c. false

Venial

In the realm of moral dilemmas, sins of a venial nature were considered minor transgressions, easily excusable, and lacking grave consequences. These slight infractions, though not to be dismissed, did not carry the weight of mortal sins, and could be absolved through repentance and divine mercy. The penitent soul sought redemption, hoping that his minor sins would not hinder his path to spiritual growth.

Venial means:

a. mortal   b. grave   c. forgivable

Artisan

Skilled in the meticulous craft of their trade, they were the masters of their respective domains. The artisans hands deftly shaped raw materials into exquisite pieces of art, showcasing their talent and dedication. Each creation was a testament to their expertise, reflecting their commitment to preserving traditional techniques.

Artisan means:

a. amateur   b. novice   c. craftsman

Coddle

In the nurturing embrace of a mother's love, she would coddle her newborn, tenderly cradling the delicate bundle in her arms. She would dote on every whimper and sigh, providing warmth, comfort, and protection. With unwavering devotion, she sought to ensure her child's well-being and foster an environment of unbridled affection.

Coddle means:

a. neglect   b. pamper   c. mistreat

Disseminating

In the age of information, the internet served as an exceptional tool for disseminating knowledge to the masses. Ideas, research findings, and intellectual insights were shared at an unprecedented speed, transcending geographical boundaries. The power of dissemination lies in its capacity to empower individuals, enlightening minds and fueling discourse.

Disseminating means:

a. concealing   b. spreading   c. hoarding

Fortitude

Amidst the trials and tribulations of life, one's fortitude emerged as a defining trait, demonstrating strength of character in the face of adversity. It was the unwavering resolve, the courage that propelled individuals forward, enabling them to confront challenges head-on. With endurance as their guiding force, they persevered, undeterred by the obstacles that lay in their path.

Fortitude means:

a. resilience   b. weakness   c. frailty

Innocuous

Within the tranquil garden, the butterfly flitted gracefully from flower to flower, its innocent presence adding an aura of serenity. Unbeknownst to the fragile creature, its colorful wings carried no harm, bringing joy and wonder to those who beheld its beauty. The seemingly innocuous butterfly reminded us of the profound impact that small acts of kindness and simplicity could have in a complex world.

Innocuous means:

a. harmless   b. toxic   c. dangerous

Metaphorically

In literature, metaphors act as artistic devices that add depth and richness to the written word. Metaphorically speaking, these figurative expressions transcend literal meanings, initiating a dance of imagination and interpretation in the reader's mind. The metaphor breath life into the narrative, evoking emotions and painting vivid mental images that linger long after the words have been read.

Metaphorically means:

a. figuratively   b. literally   c. directly

Peerless

In a world brimming with talent and achievement, occasionally emerged individuals whose prowess knew no bounds. They were undeniably peerless, standing above the rest in their field through a combination of exceptional skill, unwavering dedication, and relentless pursuit of excellence. Their work served as a testament to the heights that could be reached when one dared to surpass mediocrity.

Peerless means:

a. unmatched   b. average   c. unremarkable

Prudent

A prudent approach is deemed essential for navigating life's complexities. A judicious individual exercise careful judgment, analyzing risks and weighing potential outcomes before taking action. He embraces foresight and sound reasoning, heedful of the consequences that may arise, ensuring that his choices are grounded in wisdom and consideration.

Prudent means:

a. cautious   b. reckless   c. impulsive

Speckled

Nature possesses a mesmerizing palette, where vibrant hues intertwined to create breathtaking spectacles. Within this tapestry of colors, the speckled patterns sprinkle across a bird's feathers or a snake's skin added a touch of mesmerizing beauty. These markings are a testament to the intricate designs crafted by evolution, adorning creatures with an exquisite visual allure.

Speckled means:

a. spotted   b. solid   c. uniform

Veracity

In storytelling and journalism, the pursuit of truth stood as an unwavering principle. The veracity of facts ensured the credibility and authenticity of accounts, allowing readers to trust in the information presented. It was through rigorous investigation and diligent reporting that journalists strove to uphold the highest standard of integrity in their work.

Veracity means:

a. dishonesty   b. truthfulness   c. deception

Ascetic

In a world driven by materialism and excess, the ascetic individual sought solace in simplicity and self-discipline. Renouncing worldly possessions and embracing a life of austerity, he transcended the allure of decadence and focused on spiritual growth. His lifestyle served as a testament to the power of inner strength and detachment from worldly desires.

Ascetic means:

a. indulgent   b. austere   c. luxurious

Coercion

Throughout history, the exercise of power has taken various forms, and one prevalent method is coercion. It involves the manipulation or assertive persuasion of others against their will, and has been used to achieve numerous aims, from political dominance to social conformity. However, it is important to recognize that the long-term effects of it often result in resentment and resistance, as individuals yearn for autonomy and freedom of choice.

Coercion means:

a. force   b. persuasion   c. consent

Diurnal

Within the natural world, diurnal creatures are those whose activities primarily occur during daylight hours. This characteristic distinguishes them from their nocturnal counterparts, who thrive under the cover of darkness. These animals have adapted to the bright light and warmth of the sun, aligning their behavior and biological rhythms with the natural cycle of day and night.

Diurnal means:

a. daytime   b. nocturnal   c. dark

Fortuitous

Life is a tapestry woven with both careful planning and unexpected occurrences. Fortuitous events, marked by chance or luck, often catch us by surprise and can deeply impact our paths. These serendipitous encounters can alter the course of our lives, granting unforeseen opportunities and forging connections that may shape our future endeavors.

Fortuitous means:

a. intentionally   b. deliberate   c. fortunate

Innovate

In the ever-evolving landscape of technology and human progress, innovation stands as a driving force behind societal advancements. To innovate is to introduce novel ideas, methods, or products that disrupt the status quo and propel humanity forward. It requires boldness, creativity, and a willingness to challenge conventional thinking, ultimately reshaping the world in remarkable ways.

Innovate means:

a. maintain   b. invent   c. stagnate

Meticulous

Precision and attention to detail are the hallmarks of a meticulous individual. Their methodical approach allows for the thorough examination and execution of tasks, leaving no room for error or oversight. Whether it be in art, science, or everyday endeavors, this person's commitment to excellence ensures that every aspect is carefully considered and executed with utmost care.

Meticulous means:

a. careful   b. careless   c. sloppy

Pejorative

Language possesses immense power, capable of shaping perceptions and influencing societal norms. The use of pejorative language, which employs derogatory or belittling terms, can be harmful, perpetuating stereotypes and diminishing the worth of individuals or groups. It is crucial to cultivate a mindset that values respectful and inclusive communication while rejecting the use of dyslogistic speech.

Pejorative means:

a. derogatory   b. affirming   c. praising

Puerile

Puerile ideas, characterized by their immaturity and lack of depth, often stem from a limited understanding or a refusal to engage with complexity. While such ideas may be prevalent during adolescence, it is crucial for individuals to embark on a journey of intellectual growth and transcend the puerile notions that once shaped their perspectives.

Puerile means:

a. childish   b. mature   c. insightful

Sporadic

Life is a series of ebbs and flows, with moments of consistency juxtaposed against fitful occurrences. Sporadic phenomena, marked by their irregular and unpredictable nature, disrupt the otherwise steady rhythm of existence. They remind us that life's inherent diversity and unpredictability can bring both excitement and challenges, as unexpected events shape our paths.

Sporadic means:

a. intermittent   b. constant   c. regular

Verbose

The art of effective communication lies in the ability to convey ideas succinctly and with clarity. However, some individuals, driven by a desire to impress or a propensity for excessive elaboration, fall victim to verbosity. Their long-winded expressions often drown the essence of their message, obscuring it under a deluge of unnecessary words.

Verbose means:

a. wordy   b. concise   c. succinct

Assiduous

In the pursuit of excellence, the meticulous individual stands firm in their commitment to thoroughness and purpose. Guided by a strong work ethic and relentless dedication, they approach tasks with unwavering focus and attention to detail. Through their assiduous efforts, they unlock the path to achieving remarkable outcomes.

Assiduous means:

a. diligently   b. lazy   c. indifferent

Cogent

In a persuasive argumentation, credibility reigns supreme. A cogent argument possesses the power to sway opinions through its logical coherence and compelling evidence. It navigates the intricacies of complex issues, presenting a clear and compelling case that leaves little room for doubt or disputation.

Cogent means:

a. weak   b. convincing   c. illogical

Divert

Throughout life, unexpected detours often emerge, presenting us with opportunities to divert from our original path. The act of diversion, characterized by a shift, can bring forth new experiences, perspectives, and avenues for growth. Embracing these diversions exposes us to a world of possibility, leading to newfound horizons of exploration and self-discovery.

Divert means:

a. redirect   b. continue   c. adhere

Fractious

Within the dynamics of social interactions, individuals may encounter those who exhibit a cranky disposition, marked by a tendency towards irritable and quarrelsome behavior. Their incessant discontent and propensity for discord disrupt the harmony that exists within social circles, leaving those around them in a state of discomfort and unease. It becomes essential to navigate the complexities of dealing with such fractious individuals, employing empathy and diplomacy to foster understanding and resolve conflicts.

Fractious means:

a. agreeable   b. irritable   c. easygoing

Inscrutable

In human nature exist individuals whose thoughts and intentions remain inscrutable, shrouded in an enigmatic veil. Their elusive nature and cryptic demeanor defy comprehension, making them a subject of intrigue and fascination. Attempting to decipher the inscrutable requires an astute observation of verbal and nonverbal cues, while acknowledging the inherent mysteriousness that may never fully unravel.

Inscrutable means:

a. enigmatic   b. clear   c. accessible

Mettle

In the face of adversity, the bravery of an individual is truly tested. It is during these challenging moments that one's true character and resolve shine through. Mettle, characterized by unwavering determination, resilience, and courage, allows individuals to tackle obstacles head-on and persevere, even in the most daunting circumstances.

Mettle means:

a. resilience   b. cowardice   c. timidity

Pellucid

In the pursuit of knowledge, clarity and lucidity are essential in the process of comprehension. The pellucid nature of information and explanations facilitates a deeper understanding, allowing individuals to grasp complex concepts with ease. Through the cultivation of a pellucid teaching style, educators have the power to illuminate minds and unlock the potential within their students.

Pellucid means:

a. clear   b. opaque   c. unclear

Punctilious

Take for instance professional conduct: there exists a standard of punctilious behavior that exemplifies meticulous attention to detail and adherence to rules and protocols. These individuals leave no room for error or oversight in their pursuit of excellence, as they exactly follow guidelines and ensure accuracy throughout their work.

Punctilious means:

a. negligent   b. meticulously   c. sloppy

Spurious

Amidst the sea of information that pervades our digital age lies the danger of encountering spurious claims and fake news. Specious information, characterized by its false and misleading nature, can sow seeds of confusion and mistrust. It is crucial for individuals to exercise critical thinking and discernment, distinguishing fact from fiction to navigate the vast landscape of knowledge.

Spurious means:

a. false   b. true   c. authentic

Verbosity

Sometimes, in communication, individuals may succumb to the allure of verbosity, indulging in an excessive use of words that veers away from terseness and conciseness. Their loquacious tendencies, often devoid of substance, can impede effective understanding and dull the impact of their intended message. It is essential to recognize the value of succinctness, ensuring that every word spoken or written resonates with clarity and purpose.

Verbosity means:

a. loquacity   b. brevity   c. conciseness

Assuage

In the face of emotional turmoil and psychological distress, individuals yearn for solace and a means to assuage their inner pain. Compassionate support, gentle reassurance, and empathetic understanding can serve as an antidote for their wounded souls. By extending a helping hand and creating a nurturing environment, one can assist in alleviating suffering and fostering a sense of peace.

Assuage means:

a. alleviate   b. intensify   c. aggravate

Cogitate

The human mind, a complex entity capable of profound contemplation, possesses the power to cogitate on matters of great significance. Through deep introspection and thoughtful analysis, individuals engage in a mental discourse that explores diverse perspectives and seeks clarity. Harnessing the ability to think empowers individuals to make informed decisions and unravel the intricate complexities of life.

Cogitate means:

a. ponder   b. neglect   c. overlook

Docile

In education and training, a docile learner is an invaluable asset. With a receptive and compliant disposition, such individuals eagerly embrace new knowledge and eagerly engage in the learning process. Docility, accompanied by an openness to instruction and adaptability, facilitates seamless cooperation and ensures a harmonious learning environment.

Docile means:

a. defiant   b. rebellious   c. compliant

Fraudulent

Amidst the intricate web of commerce and financial transactions, individuals must remain vigilant against the perils of fraudulent practices. Dishonest schemes, designed to manipulate and exploit unsuspecting victims, pose a significant threat to financial security. By cultivating a sense of skepticism and engaging in due diligence, individuals can fortify their defenses against deceitful endeavors.

Fraudulent means:

a. deceptive   b. honest   c. genuine

Insentient

In life, human sometimes lacks the capacity for lifeless perception and awareness. Insentient entities, devoid of sentient experiences, navigate the world driven by instinct and preprogrammed behaviors. Their existence serves as a reminder of the intricate spectrum of sentience that encompasses the natural world, highlighting the awe-inspiring diversity and complexity of life.

Insentient means:

a. conscious   b. awareness   c. unconscious

Milieu

In the vibrancy of a bustling metropolis, diverse cultures intermingle, each contributing its distinctive flavor to the collective identity of the city. The streets come alive, teeming with a melange of languages and customs, creating an atmosphere of constant interaction and discovery. Amidst this rich tapestry, individuals find themselves immersed in a captivating milieu that encourages personal growth and fosters a sense of belonging.

Milieu means:

a. environment   b. isolation   c. solitude

Pensive

Under the shade of a willow tree, the solitary figure sat in deep contemplation, his countenance reflecting a profound pensiveness. Thoughts meandered through the corridors of his mind, reaching deep into the recesses of his being. Lost in introspection, he sought answers to the profound questions that stirred his soul, yearning for clarity and understanding.

Pensive means:

a. carefree   b. reflective   c. distracted

Purloin

In the dimly lit gallery, a stealthy figure moved with grace, silently navigating the labyrinth of priceless artwork. With deft fingers and an astute eye, the art thief proceeded to purloin a small, exquisite painting, its absence yet to be noticed by unsuspecting guardians. Breathing a sigh of relief, the thief vanished into the night, leaving behind a sense of loss and betrayal.

Purloin means:

a. steal   b. return   c. give

Stagnant

Within the depths of the moribund pond, a thick layer of algae covered the placid surface, suffocating the life within. The absence of movement and circulation rendered the environment inhospitable, devoid of vitality. Time stood still in this lifeless expanse, as nature's rhythm faltered amidst the stagnation that gripped the once thriving habitat.

Stagnant means:

a. dynamic   b. still   c. vibrant

Vertigo

As the acrobat gracefully twirled through the air, the audience was captivated by a sense of awe and wonder, accompanied by a tingling sensation of vertigo. Suspended at great heights, defying gravity with each daring maneuver, the performer elicited a visceral response from the crowd, inspiring a combination of admiration and trepidation.

Vertigo means:

a. dizziness   b. balance   c. equilibrium

Astute

Throughout business negotiations, an astute entrepreneur possesses a keen intellect and a shrewd ability to discern advantageous opportunities. With calculated precision and insightful intuition, he navigate the intricate and rapidly evolving landscape of commerce. His insightful decision-making and strategic planning lead to success and carve a path towards sustained prosperity.

Astute means:

a. naïve   b. obtuse   c. perceptive

Collage

In the art studio, the aspiring artist meticulously arranged various images, textures, and colors, creating a vibrant picture that captured the essence of her creative vision. Each carefully selected piece, whether a torn photograph or a snippet of fabric, contributed to the cohesive whole, telling a story of interconnectedness and diversity. As the final brushstroke added depth and dimension, the collage stood as a testament to the artist's ingenuity and skill.

Collage means:

a. mosaic   b. separate   c. single

Dogmatic

With unwavering conviction, the charismatic speaker disseminated her dogmatic beliefs, authoritative in their proclamation of absolute truth. Her words echoed through the crowded auditorium, invoking a sense of reverence and compliance among their followers. However, some discerning minds questioned the inherent rigidity of such dogmatic thinking, recognizing the importance of critical inquiry and open-mindedness.

Dogmatic means:

a. opinionated   b. flexible   c. adaptable

Frivolous

Throughout the high fashion event, the runway presented an array of extravagant and frivolous designs, utterly divorced from practicality or functionality. Swathed in opulent fabrics and adorned with excessive embellishments, the models strutted with an air of pretentiousness, embodying the superficiality that permeated the industry. Yet, beneath the lavish facade, a hollowness lingered, reflecting a fundamental emptiness of substance.

Frivolous means:

a. trivial   b. meaningful   c. significant

Insipid

The uninspired dish lacked the complexity and depth of flavor, leaving the discerning palate disappointed with its insipid taste. Each bite failed to excite the senses, as blandness permeated every morsel. With a heavy heart, the diner longed for a burst of culinary creativity that would rescue the otherwise forgettable meal.

Insipid means:

a. flavorful   b. bland   c. savory

Mire

In the midst of the torrential downpour, the streets transformed into a treacherous mire of mud and filth, engulfing unsuspecting pedestrians in its murky embrace. Each step became a precarious journey, as individuals struggled against the suction of the mire, desperate to maintain their footing. Only with Herculean effort did they manage to escape the clutches of the relentless quagmire.

Mire means:

a. swamp   b. solid ground   c. firmness

Penury

Amidst the crumbling facade of an impoverished neighborhood, the residents endured a life of unrelenting penury, their meager existence characterized by hardship and poverty. From derelict homes to threadbare clothing, the circumstances of impoverishment etched despair onto the faces of its victims. Yet, within their hearts, a flicker of resilience burned, providing a glimmer of hope amidst the shadows of destitution.

Penury means:

a. deprivation   b. wealth   c. affluence

Pusillanimous

As the battle raged on, the soldier cowered behind the safety of the barricade, paralyzed by fear and a profound lack of courage. In the face of adversity, their feeble spirit succumbed to doubt and retreated from the valiant efforts of their comrades. The pusillanimous act of cowardice tainted their reputation, forever marring their legacy on the battlefield.

Pusillanimous means:

a. brave   b. timid   c. bold

Staid

Within the confines of the Victorian manor, the atmosphere exuded an air of formality and restraint, reflective of the staid nature of the aristocratic inhabitants. Meticulously arranged furniture and carefully selected artwork adorned the grand salons, where proper etiquette and decorum were paramount. However, beneath the veneer of propriety, a longing for liberation from the shackles of societal expectations dwelled silently.

Staid means:

a. sedate   b. uninhibited   c. unpredictable

Vestigial

In the labyrinthine halls of the natural history museum, preserved fossils showcased the remnants of extinct creatures, their vestigial structures hinting at the evolutionary journey of life on Earth. The presence of tiny limbs in snakes and rudimentary wings in flightless birds bore testimony to the remnants of ancestral adaptations. Although vestigial, these remnants served as tangible reminders of the interconnectedness and shared history of all living organisms.

Vestigial means:

a. developed   b. rudimentary   c. evolved

Asylum

Seeking refuge from the chaos of war, the displaced refugees clung to the hope of finding it within the borders of a foreign land, where they could rebuild their shattered lives and escape the horrors they had endured. The promise of safety within the walls of an asylum offered solace and respite from the relentless hardships they faced. Within those compassionate walls, they yearned to find a sense of belonging once more.

Asylum means:

a. sanctuary   b. chaos   c. unrest

Collate

Amidst the overflowing stacks of papers and scattered documents, the diligent office worker painstakingly collated the myriad information, meticulously organizing it into coherent files. Each page was methodically arranged, ensuring seamless navigation and efficient access to vital data. With every document in its rightful place, the collation process revealed a harmonious synergy, fostering an environment of productivity and order.

Collate means:

a. scatter   b. jumble   c. compile

Dolt

In the hushed lecture hall, the professor's erudite discourse clashed against the deafening silence that enveloped the doltish students sitting in the back row. Their vacant gaze and lack of comprehension betrayed their intellectual limitations, eliciting both frustration and pity from their peers. Despite the professor's best efforts to engage and enlighten, the dolts remained impervious to the glimmer of knowledge that danced before them.

Dolt means:

a. genius   b. idiot   c. prodigy

Frugal

In the quaint cottage nestled amidst the rolling hills, the frugal couple embraced a modest lifestyle, carefully calculating their every expense and avoiding unnecessary extravagance. They sought comfort in a simple existence, finding joy in the warmth of shared moments rather than material possessions. Their prudent financial habits and mindful choices allowed them to cultivate a life filled with contentment and financial stability.

Frugal means:

a. thrifty   b. lavish   c. wasteful

Instigate

With a devious glint in his eyes, the cunning manipulator schemed and plotted, seeking to instigate discord and chaos within the otherwise peaceful community. His deceptive words and clever maneuvers successfully sparked tensions among once-trusted allies, pitting them against each other in a web of enmity. With each calculated move, he observed the consequences of his actions unfold, reveling in the havoc he had incited.

Instigate means:

a. pacify   b. provoke   c. reconcile

Misanthrope

Sitting alone on the park bench, the misanthrope observed the bustling crowd with a disdainful gaze, shunning the company of his fellow human beings. Intensely skeptical of their motives and disillusioned by their inherent flaws, he retreated into a self-imposed solitude, finding solace in the unbiased embrace of nature instead. His isolation became the defining characteristic of his existence, shielding him from the disappointments that human interactions often brought.

Misanthrope means:
a. humanitarian   b. sociable   c. cynic

Perceptive

With an astute mind and keen observation skills, the detective pieced together the fragments of evidence, uncovering the hidden truths that lay masked beneath the surface. Every subtle gesture, every fleeting expression held significance to her discerning eye, allowing her to decipher the intricate web of lies and deception. Through her unwavering dedication, the perceptive detective brought justice to the perplexing case that had confounded others.

Perceptive means:
a. observant   b. oblivious   c. obtuse

Pyromania

Deep within the troubled psyche of the arsonist, a dangerous obsession with fire raged uncontrollably, driving him to ignite destructive blazes wherever he went. The alluring dance of the flames and the destruction he left in his wake provided a twisted satisfaction that temporarily mollified his inner turmoil. Consumed by his pyromania, the arsonist found solace in the chaos he wreaked, only to be ultimately consumed by his own fiery desires.

Pyromania means:
a. firebug   b. fire safety   c. fire extinguisher

Stanza

Within the poetic symphony of words, each carefully crafted stanza painted a vivid picture, weaving emotions and imagery into a tapestry of verse. The rhythmic cadence and melodic flow captivated the readers' senses, immersing them in the poet's profound introspection. As the final stanza cascaded onto the page, the poet's message resonated deeply, leaving an indelible mark on the hearts and minds of those who dared to delve into their poetic world.

Stanza means:
a. verse   b. prose   c. sentence

Vignette

Amidst the bustling city streets, a vignette unfolded, capturing a brief, yet poignant snapshot of humanity. In this fleeting moment, the weary artist observed a passerby, etching their essence onto the canvas of his mind. A symphony of emotions swirled within the vignette, an intricate blend of joy, sorrow, and vulnerability, forming a timeless portrait of the human experience.

Vignette means:

a. epic   b. sketch   c. saga

Atheist

Within the scope of philosophical discourse, he critically questioned the existence of a divine being, rejecting the notion of a transcendent force governing the universe. Through careful analysis and rational thought, he grappled with the complexities of faith and reason, seeking to uncover the fundamental truths that underpin their worldview. The atheist's unwavering skepticism rendered them both an enigma and a beacon of intellectual curiosity.

Atheist means:

a. nonbeliever   b. theist   c. devout

Colloquial

Amidst the lively chatter of the local marketplace, a rich tapestry of colloquial expressions filled the air, painting a vivid picture of cultural identity and shared experiences. The familiar phrases and informal slang forged an instant connection between strangers, bridging the gap between diverse backgrounds and fostering a sense of camaraderie. Through the lens of casual language, the vibrant pulse of the community was brought to life.

Colloquial means:

a. informal   b. formal   c. proper

Dotard

As old age descended upon him like a relentless tide, the once eminent professor found himself battling an insidious foe: the eroding faculties of his mind. Once revered for his intellectual prowess, he was reduced to a dotard, struggling to recall the words and ideas that once flowed effortlessly from his being. Despite this cruel fate, his enduring spirit and indomitable willpower shone through, inspiring those around him with his unwavering determination.

Dotard means:

a. senile   b. lucid   c. astute

Furrow

Under the scorching sun, the farmer relentlessly toiled, sweat dripping down his brow as he relentlessly plowed his land, creating neat trenches that would soon cradle the seeds of tomorrow's harvest. The rhythmic motion of his labors reflected the resilience and dedication ingrained in his very being. Each furrow served as a testament to his unwavering commitment to providing sustenance for his community.

Furrow means:
a. smooth   b. groove   c. even

Instigator

Within the heated debate, an instigator's cunning words and strategic actions sparked a chain reaction of tension, causing the once peaceful gathering to descend into chaos. His deliberate provocations and manipulation sowed the seeds of dissent, turning friends into foes and tearing apart the fragile fabric of unity. He reveled in the discord they had engineered, his agenda shrouded in a cloak of secrecy.

Instigator means:
a. provocateur   b. mediator   c. pacifier

Misnomer

In art, the term "abstract" is often deemed a misnomer, for it failed to encapsulate the intricate emotions and complex narratives contained within these unconventional masterpieces. Critics argued that labeling such works as "abstract" undermined their true essence, as they defied categorization and spoke to the depths of the human experience. Though called "abstract," these paintings revealed a profound reality that surpassed mere representation.

Misnomer means:
a. misidentification   b. accurate name   c. precise label

Percipient

With a keen eye for detail, the detective surveyed the crime scene, meticulously scanning for any clue that would unravel the enigma before them. His astute observations and intuitive deductions painted a vivid picture of the events that had transpired, piecing together the fragmented fragments of truth. In the face of adversity, the investigator remained steadfast, his unwavering determination leading him towards the path of justice.

Percipient means:
a. perceptive   b. unaware   c. oblivious

Quaff

Amidst the jubilant festivities, the revelers raised their glasses, eager to quaff the effervescent elixir that flowed freely, indulging in its intoxicating embrace. The golden liquid cascaded down their throats, igniting a symphony of sensations that danced upon their palates. As they savored each drop, the quaff transformed into a celebration of life, forging bonds of camaraderie and immortalizing moments of bliss.

Quaff means:

a. drink   b. abstain   c. eschew

Staunch

In politics, they fought tirelessly for the rights of the marginalized, an unwavering champion of justice in the face of adversity. Their unwavering commitment to their cause stirred a fire within their followers, igniting hope and inspiring others to join the battle against inequality. The staunch advocates, undeterred by the challenges that lay ahead, proclaimed their unwavering support for those who had long been silenced.

Staunch means:

a. wavering   b. flexible   c. steadfast

Vilification

The power of vilification is a formidable weapon, employed by those seeking to tarnish the reputation of their rivals. Through a relentless barrage of slanderous accusations and malicious rumors, they aimed to destroy the credibility and integrity of their adversaries. This vicious cycle perpetuated a culture of distrust and animosity, poisoning the very essence of civil discourse.

Vilification means:

a. praise   b. accolade   c. defamation

Atrophy

In the area of physical fitness, a sedentary lifestyle served as a breeding ground for the weakening of muscles and the decline of overall health. Lack of exercise and a failure to engage in regular movement caused the body to languish and deteriorate, leaving individuals weakened and vulnerable. Only through consistent and targeted physical activity could one hope to reverse the effects of atrophy and restore vitality to their being.

Atrophy means:

a. wasting   b. growth   c. development

Collusion

In the treacherous world of politics, the shadows concealed a web of agreements, where powerful figures conspired in hushed tones to manipulate the course of democracy. Behind closed doors, secret alliances were forged, birthing a sinister dance of deceit and hidden agendas. The true extent of this collusion remained shrouded in darkness, ensnaring the innocent in a web of manipulation and betrayal.

Collusion means:

a. transparency   b. conspiracy   c. honesty

Drawl

In the Southern countryside, time seemed to slow as the inhabitants embraced the languid accent that painted their speech with rich melodies. Each word rolled lazily off their tongues, adorned with the cadence of the warm summer breeze. The drawl, a reflection of their cultural heritage, breathed life into their stories, infusing them with a sense of the unhurried rhythm of the land.

Drawl means:

a. twang   b. articulation   c. enunciation

Furtive

In the dimly lit alleyways, a furtive figure skulked, its presence masked by the cloak of darkness. its movements were swift and calculated, betraying an air of secrecy and hidden intent. As it disappeared into the night, its presence left a lingering sense of unease, a subtle reminder of the lurking dangers that resided in the shadows.

Furtive means:

a. clandestine   b. overt   c. open

Insurgent

In the heart of the conflict-stricken region, a defiant voice arose, rallying the oppressed masses against their oppressors. The insurgent harnessed the power of dissent, his impassioned speeches igniting a flicker of rebellion in the hearts of the disenfranchised. With each act of defiance, he chipped away at the foundations of the oppressive regime, offering a glimmer of hope in a world trapped in chaos.

Insurgent means:

a. rebel   b. loyalist   c. follower

Misogynist

With every derogatory remark, he sowed seeds of discrimination and hatred, fueling a toxic environment for women. his deeply ingrained prejudice tainted every interaction, perpetuating the cycle of gender-based oppression. The pain inflicted by the misogynist's words resonated deeply, serving as a reminder of the battles still fought for gender equality.

Misogynist means:

a. sexist   b. feminist   c. egalitarian

Perdition

In the depths of despair, the lost soul faced the grim reality of his choices, teetering on the precipice of perdition. His actions, driven by greed and selfishness, had led him down a path of self-destruction. As he peered into the abyss, the weight of his sins became undeniable, pushing him closer to the brink of eternal damnation.

Perdition means:

a. damnation   b. salvation   c. redemption

Quagmire

As the rain poured relentlessly, transforming the once grassy path into a treacherous quagmire, the hiker found themselves trapped in nature's muddy embrace. Each step became an arduous struggle against the suctioning grip of the difficult terrain. In this boggy swamp, his hopes of reaching safety seemed to fade away.

Quagmire means:

a. marsh   b. dry land   c. solid footing

Stereotype

In a world brimming with diversity, the weight of cliché lay heavy upon the shoulders of individuals who did not conform to society's expectations. These preconceived notions cast unyielding shadows, coloring perceptions and limiting the potential of those deemed outsiders. It was only through acceptance and understanding that the shackles of stereotype could be shattered.

Stereotype means:

a. generalization   b. uniqueness   c. acceptance

Vindicate

With every piece of evidence presented, the lawyer's meticulous arguments began to weave a tapestry of truth that could not be denied. The accused, once burdened by false accusations, now found solace in the steadily mounting evidence that would vindicate their name. As the verdict was announced, justice prevailed, vindicating the innocent with resolute finality.

Vindicate means:
a. exonerate   b. incriminate   c. blame

Attenuate

Through the dense foliage, the sunlight weaved its way, casting a glow upon the forest floor. The droplets of rain that lingered on the leaves delicately refracted the light, creating a shimmering spectacle of nature's beauty. In this attenuated illumination, the tranquility of the woods seemed to come alive.

Attenuate means:
a. strengthen   b. weaken   c. intensify

Commandeer

Amidst the chaos of battle, the commander's voice boomed, barking orders to his troops. With unwavering authority, he sought to commandeer the strategic advantage and turn the tides of war. His vision and leadership ignited a surge of determination within his soldiers, propelling them forward towards victory.

Commandeer means:
a. relinquish   b. take over   c. yield

Drivel

The once captivating debate devolved into an exchange of nonsensical gibberish, as the speakers failed to present any substantial arguments. Their words, devoid of logical coherence, seemed to elicit more confusion than enlightenment. It was through critical thinking and discernment that one could sift through the drivel and uncover the nuggets of wisdom buried within.

Drivel means:
a. eloquence   b. nonsense   c. articulation

Futile

With trembling hands, she tirelessly attempted to unlock the intricately designed puzzle box, each futile attempt only deepening the frustration etched upon her face. Hours turned into days, as the seemingly impenetrable mechanisms defied her every effort. Finally, with a defeated sigh, she realized her endeavors were in vain.

Futile means:

a. effective   b. pointless   c. productive

Interminable

The sound of the clock's monotonous ticking echoed through the empty room, stretching the passing seconds into an interminable expanse of time. Every minute seemed to linger, refusing to concede to the next. As boredom settled in, the student found themselves trapped in this never-ending lecture, longing for its conclusion.

Interminable means:

a. endless   b. fleeting   c. finite

Misrepresentation

In politics, words served as both powerful weapons and treacherous traps. Through careful manipulation and selective omissions, politicians wove a web of deceit to sway public opinion. However, when the truth was unveiled, the people demanded justice for the deceptive misrepresentation that had clouded their judgment.

Misrepresentation means:

a. distortion   b. accuracy   c. truth

Peremptory

With an authoritative tone, the supervisor issued a command, leaving no room for negotiation or compromise. The force of his words silenced any opposing voices, establishing his dominance and control. In this peremptory manner, decisions were made, and actions were taken, leaving little room for dissent.

Peremptory means:

a. decisive   b. flexible   c. lenient

Quaint

Nestled amidst rolling hills, the village stood frozen in time, its charm capturing the imaginations of all who visited. Cobblestone streets meandered past centuries-old cottages, their thatched roofs a testament to a bygone era. In this quaint hamlet, the whispers of history whispered through the air.

Quaint means:

a. modern   b. contemporary   c. picturesque

Stevedore

With brawny arms and unwavering determination, the stevedore tirelessly unloaded cargo from the massive shipping vessel. Each crate, heavy with its own secrets, met its fate at the hands of these industrious workers. Through their perseverance and skill, they ensured the smooth and efficient flow of goods into the harbor.

Stevedore means:

a. dockworker   b. office worker   c. manager

Virtuoso

As the orchestra filled the grand concert hall with a symphony of harmonious melodies, the pianist took center stage, his nimble fingers gliding across the keys in a breathtaking display of virtuosity. Each note he played showcased his exceptional skill and mastery of the instrument, leaving the audience in awe of his talent. The virtuoso's performance culminated in a thunderous applause that reverberated throughout the hall.

Virtuoso means:

a. prodigy   b. amateur   c. beginner

Augment

Driven by a desire for improvement, the scientist tirelessly sought ways to augment the capabilities of the existing technology. Through countless hours of research and experimentation, she discovered innovative methods to amplify its functionality and broaden its scope. With her breakthrough, she could finally increase the efficiency of the machine.

Augment means:

a. enhance   b. reduce   c. minimize

Complacent

Having achieved success early in life, the young entrepreneur grew complacent and content with his accomplishments. He became indifferent to the ever-changing landscape of his industry, oblivious to the potential threats and new opportunities that lay ahead. It was only when He faced significant setbacks that his complacency shattered, revealing the need for renewed drive and determination.

Complacent means:

a. satisfied   b. driven   c. ambitious

Droll

With a mischievous grin, the comedians charmed the audience with their sense of humor, infusing each joke with unexpected wit and satire. Laughter filled the room as their comedic timing and clever wordplay tickled the funny bones of all who listened. The droll punchline left the crowd in stitches.

Droll means:

a. amusing   b. serious   c. solemn

Galleon

Amidst the crashing waves and salty sea breeze, the majestic galleon sailed proudly across the vast ocean, its billowing sails capturing the spirit of adventure and exploration. Laden with treasures and manned by a courageous crew, it braved the perils of the open waters in search of distant lands. The ancient galleon's voyage saw it reaching the shores of uncharted territories.

Galleon means:

a. dinghy   b. ship   c. canoe

Intermittent

The flickering candle cast irregular shadows on the worn pages of the old diary, illuminating the secrets hidden within. The author's fitful entries hinted at a life of mystery and intrigue, providing glimpses into his tumultuous journey. Each intermittent insight into his past added another layer of complexity to the enigmatic tale.

Intermittent means:

a. sporadic   b. consistent   c. continuous

Mitigate

In the face of an impending environmental crisis, scientists and policymakers collaborated to devise strategies to lessen the adverse effects of climate change. Through comprehensive research and a multidisciplinary approach, they identified measures to reduce greenhouse gas emissions and promote sustainable practices. Their diligent efforts aimed to mitigate the potential devastation caused by global warming.

Mitigate means:

a. worsen   b. alleviate   c. amplify

Perfidy

In the intricate web of political intrigue, a traitor's perfidy was exposed, shattering the trust that had once united the nation. Hidden behind a facade of loyalty, his deceitful actions undermined the stability and integrity of the government. The consequences of their betrayal would reverberate for years to come.

Perfidy means:

a. treachery   b. loyalty   c. fidelity

Quandary

Caught in a moral quandary, the protagonist was torn between honoring his personal principles and succumbing to societal expectations. The weight of his decision hung heavy on his conscience as he grappled with the conflicting options before them. Only through careful contemplation could he finally resolve his moral quandary.

Quandary means:

a. certainty   b. resolution   c. dilemma

Stifle

In a classroom filled with oppressive heat and suffocating silence, the students struggled to concentrate on their studies. The absence of fresh air and the monotonous drone of the teacher's voice threatened to stifle their enthusiasm for learning. They yearned for respite, a chance to escape the stifling environment and embrace the freedom of the outdoors.

Stifle means:

a. fostering   b. inspire   c. suppress

Virulent

The community grappled with the outbreak of a virulent disease, its rapid spread infecting countless individuals within a matter of weeks. The symptoms were severe and the mortality rate alarmingly high. Medical professionals worked tirelessly to develop treatments and contain the contagion before it could claim more lives.

Virulent means:

a. infectious   b. benign   c. mild

Auspicious

As the sun rose over the horizon, casting a warm golden glow on the landscape, the couple exchanged vows, cherishing the auspicious beginning of their lifelong journey together. Surrounded by loved ones, they embarked on their marriage with hope and optimism, believing that the omens foretold a future filled with happiness and prosperity.

Auspicious means:

a. unpromising   b. ominous   c. promising

Compliant

In a society driven by rules and regulations, individuals were expected to be conforming with the established norms and guidelines. Those who willingly adhered to the prescribed standards exhibited obedience and acquiescence in their actions, fostering a harmonious and orderly environment. The importance of being compliant became particularly evident when individuals faced repercussions for their noncompliance.

Compliant means:

a. obedient   b. defiant   c. resistant

Drone

High above, a drone soared through the sky, capturing breathtaking aerial footage of the picturesque landscape below. With its agile maneuvering and advanced technology, the drone provided a unique perspective and unparalleled access to remote and inaccessible areas. Its versatility made it an invaluable tool for various applications, from professional photography to surveillance.

Drone means:

a. unmanned aerial vehicle   b. piloted vehicle   c. manned aircraft

Gambol

On a lush green meadow, a group of lambs frolicked with unrestrained glee, engaging in playful gambols as they leaped and bounded across the grassy expanse. Their youthful energy radiated as they joyfully engaged in spontaneous movements, embodying the carefree spirit of innocence. They brought an atmosphere of pure delight to all who witnessed their exuberant play.

Gambol means:

a. frolic   b. mope   c. sulk

Intransigence

Amidst heated negotiations, the opposing parties displayed a remarkable level of intransigence, refusing to yield or compromise on their respective positions. The stubborn entrenchment in their viewpoints hindered any progress towards finding a mutually acceptable solution. Despite the mediators' best efforts, both sides resulted in a stalemate where no consensus could be reached.

Intransigence means:

a. flexibility   b. stubbornness   c. adaptability

Modicum

With mere seconds left on the clock, the underdog team players fought relentlessly against their formidable opponents to secure even a modicum of victory. Despite overwhelming odds, their unwavering determination and tactical precision allowed them to close the gap and achieve a narrow margin of success. The players celebrated their hard-fought triumph, cherishing every ounce of the hard-earned modicum of glory.

Modicum means:

a. fragment   b. plethora   c. surplus

Perfunctory

In a rush to complete their assignments, the students scribbled down perfunctory answers, devoid of depth or thoughtfulness. Their mechanical approach to the tasks at hand reflected a lack of enthusiasm or commitment, reducing their work to mere formalities. The nature of their responses stood in stark contrast to the standards of excellence expected in their academic pursuits.

Perfunctory means:

a. superficial   b. thorough   c. detailed

Quarantine

During a severe outbreak of a contagious disease, individuals who had potentially been exposed were placed under strict quarantine, isolating them from the general population to prevent further transmission. This precautionary measure aimed to curtail the spread of the pathogen and safeguard public health. Its effectiveness depended on the complete adherence of isolated individuals to the guidelines provided by health authorities.

Quarantine means:

a. freedom   b. release   c. isolation

Stoic

In the face of adversity, the stoic individual maintained a calm and composed demeanor, concealing their inner turmoil and emotions. Demonstrating a remarkable capacity for self-control, they faced life's hardships with unwavering resilience and a quiet strength. The stoic person's ability to endure suffering without complaint or display of vulnerability was both awe-inspiring and perplexing to others.

Stoic means:

a. impassive   b. volatile   c. emotional

Annex

As tensions escalated between two neighboring nations, one began preparations to annex a disputed territory, seeking to expand its own borders and exert control over the region. The annexation, executed through legal or military means, represented a strategic maneuver to extend influence and consolidate power. This aggressive act often provoked international condemnation and may lead to further destabilization.

Annex means:

a. acquire   b. relinquish   c. cede

Analgesic

The patient, wracked with excruciating pain, was administered a potent painkiller that swiftly alleviated their suffering, granting a temporary respite from agony. This powerful pain-relieving medication, targeted the sensory receptors, dulled nerve signals, and provided a soothing calmness to the afflicted individual. The relief offered by the analgesic allowed the patient to regain a measure of comfort and focus on recovery.

Analgesic means:

a. sedative   b. stimulant   c. irritant

Caucus

Party members gathered for a caucus, engaging in heated debates and deliberations on crucial matters ranging from policy decisions to candidate selections. The closed-door nature of this caucus created an environment where ideas, alliances, and strategies were fiercely contested and negotiated. Through these intense discussions, it became a pivotal event that shaped the direction and stance of the political party.

Caucus means:

a. meeting   b. dispersion   c. dissolution

Deteriorate

Over time, neglect and environmental factors caused the once pristine and elegant historic building to deteriorate, with its grandeur gradually fading away. The ravages of time and the lack of maintenance led to structural decay, crumbling facades, and a general decline in the building's overall condition. Despite efforts to preserve its former glory, the inevitable and irreparable deterioration left a poignant reminder of the impermanence of architectural wonders.

Deteriorate means:

a. decay   b. improve   c. thrive

Exposition

The renowned author skillfully crafted an elaborate exposition, setting the stage for an intricate narrative that unfolded amidst a vivid and detailed backdrop. Through meticulous descriptions and contextual information, it introduced key characters, established the story's setting, and provided essential background knowledge. As readers immersed themselves in the richly textured world, they eagerly anticipated the unfolding of the plot.

Exposition means:

a. conclusion   b. resolution   c. introduction

Incessant

The sound of raindrops on the roof created an incessant rhythm, persistently drumming against the eardrums and filling the room with a comforting white noise. The repetitive nature of the rain's patter conjured a sense of tranquility as it continued unabated, soothing the weary soul and lulling one into a peaceful state. The sound of the nonstop rain gradually merged with the background, becoming a source of solace.

Incessant means:

a. continuous   b. intermittent   c. sporadic

Alacrity

With a sense of fervor and alacrity, the ardent volunteer tackled every task assigned, diligently working with enthusiasm and a readiness to assist. Their zeal was infectious, motivating others to join in, and a vibrant sense of camaraderie flourished. The volunteer's alacrity spread like wildfire, infusing the atmosphere with a contagious energy.

Alacrity means:

a. eagerness   b. hesitancy   c. sluggishness

Burgeon

In the fertile valley, the fields burgeoned with a vibrant tapestry of flowers, a testament to the bountiful riches of nature's cycle. The once barren landscape now teemed with life as buds bloomed, petals unfurled, and colors intermingled. The incoming flora transformed the vista into a breathtaking spectacle, capturing the awe and reverence of all who beheld it.

Burgeon means:

a. decline   b. wither   c. flourish

Deleterious

The scientist's groundbreaking research exposed the deleterious effects of prolonged exposure to noxious pollutants, unveiling the hidden dangers that lurked within our environment. The data revealed a sobering truth – the pollutants wreaked havoc on both human health and ecosystems, leaving behind a trail of irreversible damage. The scientist's findings ignited a sense of urgency to address this pressing issue.

Deleterious means:

a. harmful   b. beneficial   c. constructive

Euphemism

In sensitive conversations, individuals often employed euphemisms to convey unpleasant or taboo topics in a more socially acceptable manner, delicately veiling the harsh reality with softer language. These linguistic constructs offered a veneer of politeness, minimizing offense while addressing sensitive matters with tact and subtlety. Through them, people navigated moral minefields, balancing truthfulness with diplomacy.

Euphemism means:

a. polite term   b. directness   c. bluntness

Hypocritical

In politics, where words are carefully crafted to sway public opinion, a renowned statesman emerged, known for his eloquence and persuasive speeches. Yet, behind closed doors, his actions betrayed his true nature, as he engaged in secretive dealings and double standards. The hypocrisy of his public persona became evident, tarnishing his reputation and leaving the citizens disillusioned.

Hypocritical means:

a. genuine   b. honest   c. insincere

Lethargic

Under the scorching sun, the exhausted hiker trudged along the arduous trail, every step requiring a tremendous effort. The sweltering heat and lack of water left them feeling lethargic and drained, their limbs heavy and their pace sluggish. With each passing minute, their energy waned further, until finally, they collapsed on the ground, succumbing to their extreme fatigue.

Lethargic means:

a. sluggish   b. lively   c. vigorous

Ogle

In the bustling city streets, a young woman walked with confidence, eliciting admiring glances from passersby. However, amidst the harmless gazes, a stranger's intent stare crossed the line, transforming into an unsettling ogling that made her feel objectified and vulnerable. With discomfort etched on her face, she quickened her pace, seeking refuge from the intrusive gaze.

Ogle means:

a. avert   b. disregard   c. stare

Postulate

Within the scientific community, a brilliant mind proposed a groundbreaking theory that challenged existing paradigms. Drawing upon years of research and experimentation, the scientist postulated a hypothesis that would revolutionize the field. Through rigorous testing and peer review, it stood the test of scrutiny, solidifying its place in scientific discourse.

Postulate means:

a. disprove   b. hypothesize   c. reject

Robust

In the idyllic countryside, rows of vibrant crops swayed in the gentle breeze, their sturdy stalks declaring their robustness and vitality. The fertile soil and favorable climate nurtured a bounty of fruits and vegetables, fostering a sustainable ecosystem that supported the well-being of both humans and nature. The husky harvest served as a reminder to the harmonious relationship between mankind and the land.

Robust means:

a. strong　　　　　　　　b. frail　　　　　　　　c. delicate

Tractable

Within the classroom, the attentive students eagerly soaked in the teacher's words, their receptive minds proving to be tractable to new ideas and concepts. With open minds and a willingness to learn, they embraced challenges and actively engaged in the learning process. The nature of their young minds ensured a fruitful and enriching educational experience.

Tractable means:

a. obstinate　　　　　　　　b. resistant　　　　　　　　c. compliant

750 SAT WORDS AND THEIR SYNONYMS

A

Abasement	:	humiliation, degradation, debasement
Abhor	:	detest, loathe, despise
Abrasive	:	rough, coarse, harsh
Abrogate	:	revoke, invalidate, annul
Absolution	:	forgiveness, pardon, exoneration
Abstain	:	refrain, withhold, avoid
Abstemious	:	moderate, temperate, restrained
Abstruse	:	complex, intricate, obscure
Accolade	:	honor, recognition, praise
Acquiesce	:	comply, concede, submit
Acrid	:	pungent, foul, offensive
Acrophobia	:	vertigo, height-fear, fear of heights
Acuity	:	sharpness, keenness, perception
Adamant	:	resolute, steadfast, unwavering
Adroit	:	skillful, adept, proficient
Adulation	:	praise, admiration, worship
Adversity	:	hardship, difficulty, misfortune
Advocate	:	supporter, proponent, champion
Aesthetic	:	artistic, pleasing, stylish
Affable	:	amiable, genial, cordial
Alacrity	:	eagerness, enthusiasm, willingness
Alchemy	:	sorcery, transmutation, magic
Alibi	:	excuse, justification, defense
Allay	:	alleviate, soothe, ease
Alleviate	:	relieve, mitigate, ease
Aloof	:	distant, detached, remote
Altruism	:	selflessness, philanthropy, benevolence
Amass	:	accumulate, gather, accrue
Ambiguity	:	vagueness, equivocation, obscurity
Ambiguous	:	vague, uncertain, unclear
Ambivalence	:	indecision, hesitation, doubt
Ambulatory	:	walking, mobile, roving
Ameliorate	:	improve, enhance, alleviate
Amelioration	:	improvement, betterment, enhancement
Amiable	:	affable, genial, congenial
Amity	:	friendship, harmony, goodwill
Amorphous	:	shapeless, formless, indefinite
Analgesic	:	painkiller, sedative, anodyne
Analogous	:	similar, parallel, comparable
Anarchy	:	chaos, disorder, turmoil
Anecdote	:	tale, story, narrative
Animosity	:	hostility, enmity, antagonism
Annex	:	acquire, seize, incorporate
Anomaly	:	deviation, irregularity, oddity

750 SAT WORDS AND THEIR SYNONYMS

A (continued…)

Antagonism	:	hostility, animosity, conflict
Antagonistic	:	hostile, confrontational, adversarial
Antediluvian	:	ancient, archaic, prehistoric
Anthology	:	compilation, collection, treasury
Anthropocentrism	:	human-centeredness, human supremacy, human exceptionalism
Antiquated	:	outdated, old-fashioned, obsolete
Apathetic	:	indifferent, unconcerned, uninterested
Apathy	:	indifference, detachment, unconcern
Apocryphal	:	fictitious, spurious, mythical
Appease	:	pacify, placate, soothe
Apprehensive	:	anxious, worried, uneasy
Arable	:	cultivable, fertile, productive
Arbitrary	:	random, capricious, erratic
Arcane	:	mysterious, obscure, cryptic
Archaic	:	outdated, ancient, obsolete
Archetype	:	prototype, model, exemplar
Archives	:	records, repository, collection
Articulate	:	eloquent, fluent, expressive
Artifice	:	deception, trickery, façade
Artisan	:	craftsman, maker, creator
Ascetic	:	austere, abstinent, self-denying
Assiduous	:	diligent, industrious, meticulous
Assuage	:	alleviate, mitigate, soothe
Astute	:	perceptive, insightful, discerning
Asylum	:	sanctuary, shelter, haven
Atheist	:	nonbeliever, agnostic, skeptic
Atrophy	:	wasting, degeneration, deterioration
Attenuate	:	weaken, diminish, reduce
Augment	:	enhance, expand, amplify
Auspicious	:	promising, propitious, favorable

B

Bigot	:	racist, chauvinist, dogmatist
Bilk	:	cheat, defraud, swindle
Billowing	:	surging, swelling, flapping
Blasphemy	:	sacrilege, irreverence, heresy
Blatant	:	obvious, evident, flagrant
Blighted	:	contaminated, ruined, devastated
Blithe	:	cheerful, lighthearted, carefree
Blunderbuss	:	shotgun, scattergun, musket
Bolster	:	strengthen, reinforce, fortify
Bombast	:	grandiloquence, rhetoric, magniloquence
Boorish	:	rude, uncouth, uncivilized
Bourgeois	:	middle class, affluent, prosperous
Braggart	:	show-off, narcissist, egotist
Brawny	:	muscular, robust, strong

750 SAT WORDS AND THEIR SYNONYMS

B (continued...)

Brevity	:	conciseness, succinctness, terseness
Bristle	:	bridle, prickle, stiffen
Broach	:	introduce, raise, initiate
Brusque	:	curt, blunt, abrupt
Bulwark	:	stronghold, fortress, barrier
Bureaucracy	:	administration, government, officialdom
Burgeon	:	flourish, thrive, prosper
Burnish	:	shine, buff, gloss
Buttress	:	support, brace, bolster
Byline	:	credit, attribution, acknowledgment

C

Cacophony	:	noise, clamor, din
Cajole	:	coax, persuade, manipulate
Caldron	:	cauldron, pot, kettle
Callow	:	inexperienced, naive, immature
Candid	:	frank, sincere, straightforward
Candor	:	honesty, frankness, openness
Cantankerous	:	grumpy, irritable, cranky
Capacious	:	spacious, roomy, ample
Capitulate	:	surrender, yield, submit
Carping	:	nitpicking, faultfinding, captious
Cartographer	:	mapmaker, geographer, topographer
Castigate	:	criticize, reprimand, chastise
Catharsis	:	purification, emotional release, relief
Caucus	:	meeting, assembly, conference
Caustic	:	corrosive, biting, acerbic
Cavalcade	:	procession, parade, convoy
Celerity	:	swiftness, rapidity, quickness
Censorious	:	critical, judgmental, disapproving
Censure	:	criticize, condemn, reprimand
Cerebral	:	intellectual, cognitive, mental
Certitude	:	certainty, assurance, conviction
Charlatan	:	impostor, fraud, quack
Chary	:	cautious, wary, hesitant
Chastises	:	reprimands, scolds, admonishes
Chicanery	:	deceit, deception, trickery
Chimerical	:	imaginary, fantastical, visionary
Choleric	:	irascible, hot-tempered, irritable
Chronicler	:	historian, recorder, archivist
Circuitous	:	winding, meandering, roundabout
Circumlocution	:	verbosity, periphrasis, indirectness
Circumscribe	:	restrict, confine, limit
Circumspect	:	cautious, prudent, wary
Circumvent	:	bypass, sidestep, evade
Clairvoyant	:	psychic, seer, prophetic
Clamor	:	uproar, racket, din

750 SAT WORDS AND THEIR SYNONYMS

C (continued...)

Clandestine	:	covert, hidden, secretive
Clemency	:	mercy, leniency, forgiveness
Cliché	:	stereotype, platitude, banality
Clientele	:	customers, patrons, buyers
Coalesce	:	unite, merge, blend
Coddle	:	pamper, indulge, spoil
Coercion	:	force, compulsion, duress
Cogent	:	convincing, compelling, persuasive
Cogitate	:	contemplate, ponder, ruminate
Collage	:	mosaic, montage, assemblage
Collate	:	compile, organize, gather
Colloquial	:	informal, vernacular, casual
Collusion	:	conspiracy, connivance, collaboration
Commandeer	:	seize, take over, appropriate
Complacent	:	self-satisfied, satisfied, smug
Compliant	:	obedient, submissive, conforming
Counterfeit	:	fake, forged, imitation
Covert	:	hidden, clandestine, undercover
Cower	:	cringe, recoil, quail
Credible	:	reliable, trustworthy, authentic
Creditable	:	praiseworthy, commendable, reputable
Credulous	:	trusting, naive, unsuspecting
Crepuscular	:	twilight, dim, dusky
Cringe	:	flinch, recoil, wince
Cryptic	:	mysterious, enigmatic, puzzling
Curtail	:	restrict, diminish, limit
Cynical	:	skeptical, pessimistic, doubtful

D

Debility	:	weakness, frailty, infirmity
Debunking	:	refute, disprove, invalidate
Decathlon	:	multi-sport competition, athletic contest, pentathlon
Decorum	:	propriety, etiquette, protocol
Decoy	:	lure, bait, entice
Deference	:	respect, reverence, homage
Defoliate	:	strip, denude, bare
Defunct	:	inactive, obsolete, non-functioning
Degradation	:	deterioration, decline, decay
Deleterious	:	harmful, damaging, detrimental
Deliberate	:	thoughtful, careful, intentional
Delineation	:	depiction, portrayal, representation
Demur	:	hesitate, object, dissent
Denounce	:	condemn, criticize, censure
Deplete	:	exhaust, consume, diminish
Deplore	:	condemn, lament, denounce
Depravity	:	corruption, wickedness, immorality
Deprecate	:	criticize, condemn, disapprove

750 SAT WORDS AND THEIR SYNONYMS

D (continued...)

Deride	:	ridicule, mock, scorn
Derogatory	:	disparaging, offensive, insulting
Desecrate	:	defile, violate, profane
Desecration	:	sacrilege, profanation, violation
Desist	:	cease, stop, abstain
Despondent	:	dejected, melancholy, gloomy
Destitution	:	poverty, impoverishment, penury
Deter	:	discourage, dissuade, deter
Deteriorate	:	decay, decline, worsen
Detrimental	:	harmful, damaging, destructive
Devoured	:	consume, eat up, engulf
Dexterous	:	skillful, adept, deft
Dichotomy	:	division, contrast, polarity
Didactic	:	educational, instructive, informative
Diffident	:	shy, hesitant, bashful
Digress	:	deviate, stray, wander
Dike	:	levee, embankment, barrier
Dilatory	:	procrastinating, sluggish, slow
Dilemma	:	predicament, quandary, conundrum
Dilettante	:	amateur, novice, hobbyist
Diligent	:	hardworking, industrious, conscientious
Diorama	:	tableau, model, exhibit
Dirge	:	elegy, requiem, lament
Disapprobation	:	condemnation, criticism, censure
Discern	:	perceive, distinguish, ascertain
Discord	:	disagreement, disharmony, conflict
Discordancy	:	disharmony, dissonance, cacophony
Discrepancy	:	inconsistency, disparity, variation
Discriminate	:	differentiate, segregate, distinguish
Discursiveness	:	digression, verbosity, long-windedness
Disdain	:	contempt, scorn, despise
Disinterested	:	impartial, unbiased, detached
Disparage	:	criticize, belittle, demean
Disparity	:	inequality, discrepancy, gap
Dispassionate	:	impartial, detached, objective
Disseminating	:	spreading, circulating, distributing
Diurnal	:	daytime, daylight, daily
Divert	:	convincing, compelling, persuasive
Docile	:	compliant, submissive, acquiescent
Dogmatic	:	opinionated, inflexible, doctrinaire
Dolt	:	idiot, fool, dimwit
Dotard	:	senile, demented, decrepit
Drawl	:	twang, accent, intonation
Drivel	:	nonsense, gibberish, babble
Droll	:	amusing, witty, hilarious
Drone	:	UAV (Unmanned Aerial Vehicle), quadcopter, unmanned aircraft

750 SAT WORDS AND THEIR SYNONYMS

E

Enfranchise	:	empower, grant rights, franchise
Engender	:	generate, instigate, provoke
Enhance	:	improve, heighten, amplify
Enigma	:	puzzle, mystery, riddle
Ensconce	:	settle, nestle, secure
Enshroud	:	cloak, veil, obscure
Enunciation	:	pronunciation, articulation, diction
Envenom	:	poison, contaminate, taint
Ephemeral	:	transient, fleeting, momentary
Epicure	:	connoisseur, gastronome, gourmet
Epistle	:	letter, missive, correspondence
Epistolary	:	letter-based, written, correspondence-related
Epitomized	:	embody, represent, exemplify
Equivocate	:	prevaricate, dodge, hedge
Err	:	make a mistake, blunder, stumble
Erratic	:	unpredictable, volatile, inconsistent
Esoteric	:	arcane, obscure, abstruse
Espouse	:	support, embrace, champion
Etymology	:	word origin, word history, philology
Eulogy	:	tribute, homage, memorial
Euphemism	:	polite term, substitute, understatement
Euphony	:	melody, harmony, music
Evacuate	:	vacate, empty, clear out
Exacerbate	:	worsen, aggravate, intensify
Exasperated	:	irritated, annoyed, frustrated
Exceptionable	:	objectionable, problematic, controversial
Exculpate	:	acquit, absolve, vindicate
Execrable	:	abominable, detestable, repulsive
Exegesis	:	interpretation, analysis, commentary
Exemplary	:	admirable, commendable, outstanding
Exemplify	:	represent, illustrate, demonstrate
Exhaustive	:	thorough, comprehensive, complete
Exonerates	:	absolves, acquits, vindicates
Exorcism	:	purification, purification rite, deliverance
Expatriate	:	emigrant, exile, migrant
Expedient	:	advantageous, beneficial, pragmatic
Expedite	:	accelerate, hasten, quicken
Exposition	:	introduction, prologue, preamble
Extol	:	praise, acclaim, commend
Extradite	:	surrender, repatriate, hand over
Extraneous	:	irrelevant, unnecessary, superfluous
Extrapolate	:	infer, deduce, project
Extrinsic	:	external, outside, superficial

F

Fallacious	:	false, misleading, deceptive
Falter	:	hesitate, stumble, waver

750 SAT WORDS AND THEIR SYNONYMS

F (continued...)

Fanatical	:	overzealous, passionate, fervent
Fanaticism	:	extremism, zealotry, fervor
Fastidious	:	meticulous, precise, scrupulous
Fatuous	:	foolish, senseless, absurd
Feasible	:	viable, achievable, practical
Fecund	:	fertile, fruitful, productive
Felicitous	:	fortunate, auspicious, fortunate
Fervor	:	zeal, passion, enthusiasm
Fickle	:	changeable, volatile, unpredictable
Finesse	:	skill, artistry, refinement
Fitful	:	intermittent, irregular, sporadic
Flagrant	:	blatant, outrageous, heinous
Flamboyant	:	ostentatious, showy, extravagant
Flaunt	:	display, exhibit, showcase
Flippant	:	frivolous, casual, lighthearted
Flout	:	defy, disregard, violate
Flustered	:	agitated, bewildered, confused
Fly-by-night	:	transient, transient enterprise, short-lived
Forensic	:	investigative, scientific, criminological
Fortitude	:	resilience, courage, endurance
Fortuitous	:	fortunate, serendipitous, accidental
Fractious	:	irritable, contentious, quarrelsome
Fraudulent	:	deceptive, deceitful, dishonest
Frivolous	:	trivial, inconsequential, superficial
Frugal	:	thrifty, economical, sparing
Furrow	:	groove, trench, rut
Furtive	:	clandestine, stealthy, secretive
Futile	:	fruitless, pointless, unsuccessful

G

Galleon	:	ship, vessel, cruiser
Gambol	:	frolic, romp, cavort

H

Hamper	:	hinder, obstruct, impede
Hangar	:	storage, shelter, depot
Harangue	:	diatribe, tirade, rant
Harbingers	:	indicators, heralds, signals
Hasten	:	accelerate, expedite, quicken
Haughtiness	:	arrogance, pride, conceit
Headstrong	:	stubborn, obstinate, resolute
Hedonism	:	pleasure-seeking, sensualism, epicureanism
Hedonist	:	pleasure-seeker, libertine, sybarite
Heed	:	listen, attend, observe
Heresy	:	blasphemy, dissent, rebellion

750 SAT WORDS AND THEIR SYNONYMS

H (continued…)

Hiatus	:	break, interlude, interruption
Hidebound	:	rigid, conservative, inflexible
Hieroglyphics	:	pictographs, symbols, inscriptions
Hinder	:	impede, obstruct, hamper
Histrionic	.	dramatic, theatrical, melodramatic
Hoary	:	frosty, silver-gray, aged
Hone	:	refine, improve, polish
Hyperbole	:	exaggeration, overstatement, amplification
Hypochondriac	:	worrier, hypohondriast, alarmist
Hypocritical	:	insincere, deceitful, duplicitous

I

Iconoclast	:	rebel, heretic, maverick
Idiosyncrasy	:	peculiarity, quirk, eccentricity
Ignominious	:	shameful, disgraceful, humiliating
Ignominy	:	disgrace, dishonor, humiliation
Illuminate	:	light up, brighten, enlighten
Illusory	:	deceptive, unreal, imaginary
Immoderate	:	excessive, extravagant, unrestrained
Immutable	:	unchangeable, enduring, constant
Impartial	:	unbiased, neutral, fair
Impecunious	:	penniless, destitute, impoverished
Impious	:	irreverent, sacrilegious, godless
Impoverished	:	destitute, needy, impoverished
Impromptu	:	spontaneous, extemporaneous, improvisational
Inadvertent	:	unintentional, accidental, unintended
Incantation	:	spell, enchantment, charm
Incarceration	:	imprisonment, confinement, detention
Incessant	:	continuous, relentless, nonstop
Incipient	:	beginning, initial, nascent
Inclination	:	tendency, propensity, disposition
Incoherent	:	unintelligible, confused, garbled
Incongruous	:	incompatible, mismatched, discordant
Inconsequential	:	trivial, unimportant, negligible
Inconspicuous	:	hidden, discreet, unnoticed
Indelible	:	permanent, enduring, unforgettable
Indifferent	:	unconcerned, aloof, apathetic
Indigenous	:	native, aboriginal, original
Indolence	:	laziness, inertia, slothfulness
Inductee	:	entrant, initiate, member
Indulgent	:	indulging, pampering, lenient
Inebriation	:	intoxication, drunkenness, tipsiness
Ineffable	:	indescribable, inexpressible, unutterable
Inept	:	incompetent, unskilled, clumsy
Inertia	:	inactivity, immobility, lethargy
Inevitable	:	unavoidable, certain, predetermined
Inexorable	:	relentless, unstoppable, inevitable

750 SAT WORDS AND THEIR SYNONYMS

I (continued…)

Inexpedient	:	imprudent, unwise, impractical
Infallible	:	flawless, impeccable, faultless
Infamous	:	notorious, notorious, disreputable
Infer	:	deduce, conclude, gather
Ingrate	:	ungrateful person, thankless individual, moocher
Ingénue	:	innocent, novice, novice
Inimical	:	hostile, unfriendly, antagonistic
Innate	:	inherent, natural, inherent
Innocuous	:	harmless, benign, inoffensive
Innovate	:	invent, create, revolutionize
Inscrutable	:	enigmatic, mysterious, impenetrable
Insentient	:	unconscious, unfeeling, lifeless
Insipid	:	bland, tasteless, dull
Instigate	:	provoke, incite, ignite
Instigator	:	provocateur, agitator, troublemaker
Insurgent	:	rebel, revolutionary, dissenter
Interminable	:	endless, never-ending, ceaseless
Intermittent	:	sporadic, irregular, occasional
Intransigence	:	stubbornness, inflexibility, rigidity

K

Kindle	:	ignite, spark, arouse
Knotty	:	complex, intricate, convoluted

L

Labyrinth	:	maze, puzzle, riddle
Labyrinthine	:	intricate, convoluted, complex
Laceration	:	gash, wound, cut
Lachrymose	:	tearful, weepy, mournful
Lackluster	:	dull, uninspired, mediocre
Laconic	:	concise, brief, succinct
Lamentation	:	mourning, wailing, dirge
Lampoon	:	satire, mockery, ridicule
Lance	:	spear, pike, javelin
Languid	:	lethargic, sluggish, listless
Languish	:	wither, deteriorate, decay
Larceny	:	theft, robbery, pilfering
Largess	:	generosity, bountifulness, munificence
Laud	:	acclaim, commend, extol
Lavish	:	extravagant, luxurious, sumptuous
Lax	:	lenient, relaxed, easygoing
Legend	:	myth, saga, fable
Legion	:	multitude, army, host
Lethargic	:	sluggish, weary, languid
Levity	:	buoyancy, gaiety, cheerfulness

750 SAT WORDS AND THEIR SYNONYMS

L (continued…)

Libertarian	:	individualist, free-market advocate, laissez-faire
Liniment	:	ointment, salve, balm
Lithe	:	agile, flexible, supple
Livid	:	furious, enraged, incensed
Lobbyist	:	advocate, spokesperson, influencer
Lofty	:	majestic, towering, elevated
Longevity	:	durability, longevity, permanence
Loquacious	:	talkative, verbose, garrulous
Lucid	:	clear, coherent, intelligible
Ludicrous	:	ridiculous, absurd, preposterous
Lukewarm	:	tepid, mild, indifferent
Lummox	:	oaf, clod, klutz
Luscious	:	delicious, scrumptious, delectable
Lynch	:	hang, execute, mob

M

Machinations	:	schemes, plots, maneuverings
Maelstrom	:	whirlpool, vortex, turmoil
Magnanimous	:	generous, benevolent, charitable
Magnate	:	tycoon, mogul, baron
Maladroit	:	clumsy, inept, awkward
Malady	:	illness, ailment, affliction
Malediction	:	curse, hex, spell
Malefactor	:	wrongdoer, criminal, offender
Malinger	:	feign illness, pretend, shirk
Malingerer	:	slacker, shirker, pretender
Malleable	:	pliable, adaptable, flexible
Mallet	:	hammer, gavel, pounder
Manipulatable	:	exploitable, malleable, pliable
Marred	:	blemished, tarnished, spoiled
Marshal	:	commander, organizer, leader
Marsupial	:	pouch-bearing, pouched, marsupian
Martinet	:	disciplinarian, taskmaster, authoritarian
Masochist	:	enthusiast, self-flagellant, sufferer
Matriarchy	:	female rule, matrifocal society, matricentric system
Maverick	:	nonconformist, renegade, iconoclast
Meager	:	scant, sparse, paltry
Meander	:	wander, ramble, stroll
Mellow	:	relaxed, laid-back, easygoing
Menagerie	:	zoo, collection, exhibit
Mendacious	:	dishonest, deceitful, untruthful
Mercenary	:	soldier of fortune, hired gun, hireling
Mercurial	:	volatile, fickle, unpredictable
Merge	:	combine, unite, integrate
Metaphorically	:	figuratively, symbolically, poetically
Meticulous	:	careful, thorough, precise
Mettle	:	resilience, fortitude, courage

750 SAT WORDS AND THEIR SYNONYMS

M (continued...)

Milieu	:	environment, setting, ambience
Mire	:	swamp, bog, marsh
Misanthrope	:	cynic, hermit, recluse
Misnomer	:	misidentification, misdesignation, inaccuracy
Misogynist	:	sexist, chauvinist, woman-hater
Misrepresentation	:	distortion, falsification, deceit
Mitigate	:	alleviate, lessen, reduce
Modicum	:	fragment, bit, trace

N

Noxious	:	harmful, toxic, poisonous
Nuance	:	subtlety, refinement, shading
Nullify	:	invalidate, annul, negate
Nuzzle	:	cuddle, snuggle, nestle

O

Obdurate	:	inflexible, adamant, resolute
Obfuscate	:	confuse, obscure, bewilder
Objective	:	goal, aim, purpose
Oblique	:	slanted, angled, inclined
Obliterate	:	annihilate, destroy, erase
Oblivious	:	unaware, ignorant, unconscious
Obscure	:	vague, ambiguous, mysterious
Obscured	:	hidden, concealed, clouded
Obsequious	:	servile, fawning, groveling
Obsession	:	fixation, passion, preoccupation
Obsolete	:	outdated, antiquated, outmoded
Obstreperous	:	unruly, noisy, rowdy
Obtuse	:	dull, unintelligent, slow-witted
Obviate	:	eliminate, avoid, circumvent
Odious	:	repugnant, repulsive, abhorrent
Officious	:	meddlesome, intrusive, overbearing
Ogle	:	stare, leer, gawk
Olfactory	:	smell, scent, aroma
Ominous	:	foreboding, threatening, menacing
Omnipotent	:	all-powerful, almighty, supreme
Omniscient	:	all-knowing, wise, knowledgeable
Onerous	:	burdensome, arduous, demanding
Onus	:	burden, duty, obligation
Opaque	:	murky, cloudy, unclear
Opulent	:	luxurious, lavish, extravagant
Ordain	:	consecrate, appoint, sanction
Ornate	:	elaborate, extravagant, lavish
Orthodox	:	traditional, conventional, traditionalist
Ossify	:	harden, solidify, rigidify

750 SAT WORDS AND THEIR SYNONYMS

O (continued…)

Ostentatious	:	showy, flamboyant, gaudy
Oust	:	remove, dethrone, expel
Overt	:	obvious, explicit, apparent
Overwrought	:	agitated, distressed, distraught

P

Palatable	:	delicious, tasty, delectable
Palisade	:	fence, barricade, enclosure
Palliative	:	soothing, comforting, alleviating
Pallid	:	pale, wan, colorless
Palpable	:	tangible, perceptible, evident
Panacea	:	remedy, cure-all, elixir
Paradigm	:	model, framework, pattern
Paradox	:	contradiction, enigma, puzzle
Paragon	:	epitome, model, exemplar
Paramount	:	predominant, primary, crucial
Parasite	:	leech, freeloader, moocher
Parched	:	dry, arid, dehydrated
Pariah	:	outcast, exile, reject
Parity	:	equality, equivalence, balance
Parochial	:	narrow-minded, insular, provincial
Parody	:	satire, spoof, caricature
Parry	:	deflect, counter, block
Parsimonious	:	frugal, thrifty, economical
Parsimony	:	frugality, thrift, economy
Partisan	:	supporter, advocate, enthusiast
Pathos	:	sorrow, empathy, compassion
Patron	:	supporter, sponsor, benefactor
Patronize	:	condescend, look down on, belittle
Paucity	:	scarcity, dearth, lack
Peccadillo	:	minor offense, lapse, indiscretion
Pedant	:	know-it-all, nitpicker, perfectionist
Pedestrian	:	pedestrian, ordinary, commonplace
Peerless	:	unmatched, unparalleled, incomparable
Pejorative	:	derogatory, disparaging, insulting
Pellucid	:	clear, transparent, lucid
Pensive	:	reflective, thoughtful, meditative
Penury	:	poverty, destitution, deprivation
Perceptive	:	observant, insightful, discerning
Percipient	:	perceptive, observant, insightful
Perdition	:	damnation, hell, eternal punishment
Peremptory	:	decisive, authoritative, commanding
Perfidy	:	treachery, betrayal, duplicity
Perfunctory	:	cursory, superficial, hasty
Placid	:	calm, peaceful, tranquil
Plagiarism	:	copying, infringement, piracy
Plaintiff	:	complainant, accuser, litigant

750 SAT WORDS AND THEIR SYNONYMS

P (continued...)

Plaudit	:	acclaim, praise, commendation
Plausible	:	believable, credible, reasonable
Plethora	:	abundance, profusion, multitude
Pliable	:	flexible, malleable, adaptable
Plumage	:	feathers, plumules, bird coat
Plummet	:	plunge, drop, fall
Podium	:	platform, stage, dais
Poignant	:	touching, moving, sentimental
Poised	:	confident, composed, graceful
Polemical	:	controversial, contentious, disputatious
Ponderous	:	weighty, cumbersome, unwieldy
Pontificate	:	expound, sermonize, lecture
Portend	:	foreshadow, presage, indicate
Portent	:	omen, sign, forewarning
Poseur	:	pretender, impostor, fake
Posterity	:	descendants, future generations, progeny
Posthumous	:	after-death, postmortem, after-demise
Postulate	:	hypothesize, conjecture, speculate
Potable	:	drinkable, clean, pure
Potent	:	powerful, strong, effective
Pragmatic	:	practical, sensible, realistic
Pragmatist	:	realist, practical, sensible
Preamble	:	introduction, preface, prologue
Precarious	:	unstable, uncertain, risky
Precedent	:	example, standard, guideline
Precept	:	principle, doctrine, guideline
Precinct	:	district, area, locality
Precipice	:	brink, edge, cliff
Precipitous	:	steep, sheer, abrupt
Preclude	:	prevent, hinder, inhibit
Precocious	:	advanced, gifted, talented
Predecessor	:	forerunner, precursor, antecedent
Predicament	:	dilemma, quandary, crisis
Preeminent	:	eminent, prominent, distinguished
Prerogative	:	right, privilege, authority
Prescient	:	prophetic, insightful, visionary
Presentiment	:	intuition, premonition, hunch
Presumptuous	:	arrogant, audacious, overconfident
Pretentious	:	ostentatious, affected, pompous
Prevaricate	:	deceive, lie, equivocate
Pristine	:	immaculate, untouched, unspoiled
Proclivity	:	inclination, tendency, predisposition
Procrastinate	:	delay, postpone, dawdle
Prodigal	:	extravagant, wasteful, spendthrift
Prodigious	:	extraordinary, remarkable, exceptional
Profane	:	sacrilegious, blasphemous, irreverent
Profanity	:	obscenity, vulgarity, cursing
Profound	:	deep, insightful, significant
Profundity	:	depth, profoundness, wisdom

750 SAT WORDS AND THEIR SYNONYMS

P (continued…)

Proletarian	:	working-class, laboring, blue-collar
Prolific	:	productive, creative, fruitful
Proponents	:	advocates, supporters, champions
Prosaic	:	ordinary, mundane, unremarkable
Proscribe	:	forbid, outlaw, ban
Prosody	:	meter, rhythm, intonation
Prostration	:	submission, obeisance, bowing
Protagonist	:	hero, main character, lead
Protean	:	versatile, adaptable, ever-changing
Protocol	:	etiquette, procedure, code
Protégé	:	apprentice, pupil, student
Provincial	:	rural, rustic, bucolic
Prudent	:	cautious, sensible, judicious
Puerile	:	childish, juvenile, immature
Punctilious	:	meticulous, precise, conscientious
Purloin	:	steal, pilfer, filch
Pusillanimous	:	timid, timorous, spineless
Pyromania	:	firebug, incendiary, arsonist

Q

Quaff	:	drink, imbibe, gulp
Quagmire	:	marsh, swamp, morass
Quaint	:	picturesque, charming, old-fashioned
Quandary	:	dilemma, predicament, conundrum
Quarantine	:	isolation, seclusion, confinement

R

Remuneration	:	payment, compensation, reward
Renown	:	fame, prestige, acclaim
Replete	:	full, stocked, abundant
Reprehensible	:	despicable, deplorable, immoral
Reprieve	:	respite, pardon, amnesty
Repudiate	:	reject, disown, disavow
Rescind	:	revoke, annul, repeal
Resignation	:	acceptance, surrender, acquiescence
Resolution	:	determination, resolve, commitment
Resonant	:	reverberating, vibrant, echoing
Respite	:	break, intermission, rest
Resplendent	:	dazzling, radiant, magnificent
Restorative	:	rejuvenating, revitalizing, invigorating
Retention	:	memory, recall, preservation
Reticent	:	reserved, taciturn, quiet
Retraction	:	withdrawal, recantation, correction
Revere	:	idolize, adore, respect
Riddled	:	filled, permeated, infested

750 SAT WORDS AND THEIR SYNONYMS

R (continued...)

Rife	:	prevalent, widespread, abundant
Rigor	:	strictness, precision, thoroughness
Robust	:	strong, vigorous, healthy
Rotund	:	plump, chubby, corpulent
Ruminate	:	ponder, reflect, contemplate
Ruse	:	deception, trick, stratagem

S

Saccharin	:	sweet, sugary, cloying
Sacrosanct	:	sacred, holy, inviolable
Sagacious	:	wise, astute, perceptive
Sage	:	wise, learned, knowledgeable
Salacious	:	lascivious, lewd, titillating
Sallow	:	wan, pale, sickly
Salubrious	:	healthy, wholesome, invigorating
Salutary	:	beneficial, advantageous, wholesome
Sanctimonious	:	self-righteous, holier-than-thou, hypocritical
Sanction	:	authorization, approval, permission
Sanguinary	:	bloody, gory, violent
Sanguine	:	hopeful, optimistic, positive
Sardonic	:	sarcastic, mocking, ironic
Savant	:	genius, prodigy, mastermind
Scale	:	magnitude, extent, size
Scapegoat	:	fall guy, patsy, sacrificial lamb
Scrupulous	:	meticulous, careful, thorough
Scrutinize	:	examine, analyze, inspect
Scuttle	:	scamper, scurry, dart
Seminary	:	theological school, divinity school, religious institute
Sensuous	:	sensual, voluptuous, alluring
Sentinel	:	guard, lookout, watchman
Sequester	:	isolate, separate, segregate
Serendipity	:	fortuity, luck, coincidence
Serene	:	calm, peaceful, tranquil
Serrated	:	jagged, toothed, saw-like
Servile	:	submissive, subservient, obedient
Skeptical	:	doubtful, incredulous, questioning
Skirmish	:	clash, encounter, engagement
Sluggard	:	lazy, idle, lethargic
Smelt	:	melt, fuse, refine
Smorgasbord	:	buffet, spread, array
Solace	:	comfort, consolation, support
Solicit	:	request, ask for, seek
Somnambulist	:	sleepwalker, noctambulist, somniloquist
Soothsayer	:	fortune-teller, oracle, seer
Sophomoric	:	immature, juvenile, puerile
Soporific	:	hypnotic, sedative, drowsy
Sparse	:	scarce, meager, limited

750 SAT WORDS AND THEIR SYNONYMS

S (continued…)

Specious	:	false, misleading, deceptive
Speckled	:	spotted, dotted, freckled
Sporadic	:	intermittent, irregular, occasional
Spurious	:	false, counterfeit, deceptive
Stagnant	:	still, motionless, inactive
Staid	:	sedate, conventional, traditional
Stanza	:	verse, quatrain, canto
Staunch	:	steadfast, resolute, unwavering
Stereotype	:	generalization, bias, cliché
Stevedore	:	dockworker, longshoreman, dockhand
Stifle	:	suppress, smother, suffocate
Stoic	:	impassive, composed, unflappable

T

Talisman	:	charm, amulet, lucky charm
Tangent	:	digression, deviation, aside
Tangible	:	physical, palpable, perceptible
Tardy	:	late, delayed, behind schedule
Tawdry	:	tacky, garish, vulgar
Tedium	:	monotony, boredom, ennui
Temper	:	moderate, restrain, control
Tenacious	:	persistent, relentless, dogged
Tentative	:	hesitant, unsure, cautious
Tenuous	:	fragile, precarious, delicate
Terse	:	concise, brief, pithy
Therapeutic	:	curative, remedial, healing
Thwart	:	hinder, obstruct, impede
Timorous	:	fearful, timid, apprehensive
Tirade	:	diatribe, harangue, rant
Titter	:	giggle, chuckle, snigger
Tome	:	volume, book, manuscript
Torpid	:	dormant, sluggish, inactive
Torpor	:	lethargy, sluggishness, inertia
Totter	:	teeter, wobble, stagger
Tractable	:	compliant, docile, malleable
Tranquil	:	peaceful, calm, serene
Transcribe	:	record, document, write down
Transgress	:	violate, infringe, trespass
Transient	:	temporary, fleeting, ephemeral
Traverse	:	cross, navigate, trek
Trepidation	:	anxiety, apprehension, unease
Trinket	:	knickknack, bauble, memento
Trite	:	cliché, banal, predictable
Trivial	:	insignificant, minor, unimportant
Truant	:	absentee, runaway, delinquent
Truncate	:	shorten, abbreviate, curtail
Tumult	:	commotion, uproar, chaos

750 SAT WORDS AND THEIR SYNONYMS

U

Turpitude	:	depravity, wickedness, corruption
Tyro	:	novice, beginner, neophyte
Ubiquitous	:	omnipresent, pervasive, universal
Unalloyed	:	pure, undiluted, genuine
Unctuous	:	oily, slick, sycophantic
Undermined	:	weaken, sabotage, subvert
Underscore	:	emphasize, highlight, accentuate
Unequivocal	:	clear, definite, unambiguous
Unfetter	:	liberate, free, release
Unfrock	:	defrock, dethrone, depose
Unprecedented	:	unparalleled, extraordinary, novel
Unscathed	:	unharmed, undamaged, intact
Unwitting	:	unaware, ignorant, unconscious
Upbraid	:	scold, reprimand, criticize
Uproarious	:	hilarious, boisterous, riotous
Upshot	:	result, outcome, consequence
Urbane	:	suave, polished, sophisticated
Usurp	:	seize, take over, overthrow
Utilitarian	:	pragmatic, practical, functional
Utopian	:	idealistic, idyllic, perfect

V

Vacillate	:	waver, hesitate, fluctuate
Vacuous	:	empty, shallow, vapid
Vagrant	:	homeless, tramp, drifter
Vapid	:	insipid, dull, bland
Variegated	:	diverse, multicolored, assorted
Vehemence	:	passion, intensity, fervor
Vehement	:	passionate, intense, fervent
Venal	:	corrupt, dishonest, bribable
Veneer	:	facade, surface, mask
Venerate	:	worship, adore, respect
Venial	:	forgivable, minor, excusable
Veracity	:	truthfulness, accuracy, integrity
Verbose	:	wordy, loquacious, prolix
Verbosity	:	loquacity, prolixity, long-windedness
Vertigo	:	dizziness, giddiness, lightheadedness
Vestigial	:	rudimentary, residual, atavistic
Vignette	:	sketch, glimpse, snapshot
Vilification	:	defamation, character assassination, slander
Vindicate	:	exonerate, clear, acquit
Virtuoso	:	prodigy, maestro, genius
Virulent	:	infectious, deadly, malignant
Vital	:	essential, crucial, indispensable

SOLUTIONS to THE 750 STORIES

Page 6: Abhor: a – Bigot: c – Counterfeit: a – Enfranchise: e
Page 7: Hamper: b – Kindle: a – Noxious: b – Placid: b
Page 8: Remuneration: b – Talisman: c – Abrasive: a – Bilk: b
Page 9: Covert: b – Engender: c – Hangar: b – Knotty: b –
Page 10: Nuance: b – Plagiarism: b – Renown: a – Tangent: b
Page 11: Abasement: b – Billowing: a – Cower: a – Enhance: a
Page 12: Harangue: c – Labyrinth: a – Nullify: b – Plaintiff: c
Page 13: Replete: a – Tangible: b – Abrogate: a – Blasphemy: b
Page 14: Credible: b – Enigma: c – Harbingers: a – Labyrinthine: a
Page 15: Nuzzle: a – Plaudit: a – Reprehensible: c – Tardy: a
Page 16: Absolution: c – Blatant: a – Creditable: a – Ensconce: a
Page 17: Hasten: a – Laceration: a – Obdurate: c – Plausible: a
Page 18: Reprieve: a – Tawdry: a – Abstain: b – Blighted: a
Page 19: Credulous: b – Enshroud: b – Haughtiness: b – Lachrymose: a
Page 20: Obfuscate: c – Plethora: c – Repudiate: a – Tedium: a
Page 21: Abstemious: a – Blithe: a – Crepuscular: a – Enunciation: c
Page 22: Headstrong: a – Lackluster: a – Objective: a – Pliable: b
Page 23: Rescind: b – Temper: b – Abstruse: a – Blunderbuss: b –
Page 24: Cringe: b – Envenom: b – Hedonism: a – Laconic: a
Page 25: Oblique: a – Plumage: b – Resignation: a – Tenacious: a
Page 26: Accolade: a – Bolster: c – Cryptic: a – Ephemeral: b
Page 27: Acquiesce: b – Bombast: b – Curtail: c – Epicure: a
Page 28: Heed: a – Lampoon: a – Hedonist: a – Lamentation: b
Page 29: Obliterate: a – Plummet: b – Resolution: a – Tentative: a
Page 30: Oblivious: b – Podium: c – Resonant: a – Tenuous: c
Page 31: Acrid: a – Boorish: a – Cynical: a – Epistle: b
Page 32: Heresy: a – Lance: c – Obscure: a – Poignant: a
Page 33: Respite: a – Terse: a – Acrophobia: a – Bourgeois: b
Page 34: Debility: c – Epistolary: b – Hiatus: a – Languid: b
Page 35: Obscured: b – Poised: c – Resplendent: a – Therapeutic: a
Page 36: Acuity: a – Braggart: a – Debunking: a – Epitomized: c
Page 37: Hidebound: c – Languish: c – Obsequious: a – Polemical: a
Page 38: Restorative: a – Thwart: a – Adamant: a – Brawny: b
Page 39: Decathlon: a – Equivocate: b – Hieroglyphics: b – Larceny: b
Page 40: Obsession: a – Ponderous: c – Retention: c – Timorous: b
Page 41: Adroit: b – Brevity: a – Decorum: c – Err: a
Page 42: Hinder: a – Largess: a – Obsolete: b – Pontificate: a
Page 43: Reticent: c – Tirade: c – Adulation: a – Bristle: c
Page 44: Decoy: a – Erratic: b – Histrionic: a – Laud: a
Page 45: Obstreperous: b – Portend: c – Retraction: a – Titter: a
Page 46: Adversity: a – Broach: a – Deference: a – Esoteric: a
Page 47: Hoary: c – Lavish: a – Obtuse: c – Portent: a
Page 48: Revere: a – Tome: a – Advocate: c – Brusque: b
Page 49: Defoliate: a – Espouse: a – Hone: a – Lax: b
Page 50: Obviate: a – Poseur: c – Riddled: a – Torpid: b
Page 51: Aesthetic: c – Bulwark: a – Defunct: a – Etymology: b
Page 52: Hyperbole: b – Legend: a – Odious: a – Posterity: b
Page 53: Rife: a – Torpor: c – Affable: c – Bureaucracy: a
Page 54: Degradation: c – Eulogy: a – Hypochondriac: c – Legion: b
Page 55: Officious: b – Posthumous: b – Rigor: a – Totter: a
Page 56: Alchemy: a – Burnish: c – Deliberate: b – Euphony: b
Page 57: Iconoclast: a – Levity: a – Olfactory: b – Potable: a
Page 58: Rotund: c – Tranquil: a – Alibi: a – Buttress: b

SOLUTIONS to THE 750 STORIES

Page 59: Delineation: a – Evacuate: a – Idiosyncrasy: b – Libertarian: c
Page 60: Ominous: a – Potent: c – Ruminate: a – Transcribe: c
Page 61: Allay: b – Byline: a – Demur: c – Exacerbate: a
Page 62: Ignominious: a – Liniment: a – Omnipotent: a – Pragmatic: b
Page 63: Ruse: a – Transgress: b – Alleviate: a – Cacophony: a
Page 64: Denounce: a – Exasperated: b – Ignominy: a – Lithe: a
Page 65: Omniscient: a – Pragmatist: a – Saccharin: a – Transient: c
Page 66: Aloof: a – Cajole: a – Deplete: b – Exceptionable: c
Page 67: Illuminate: b – Livid: a – Onerous: a – Preamble: a
Page 68: Sacrosanct: a – Traverse: a – Altruism: c – Caldron: a
Page 69: Deplore: b – Exculpate: a – Illusory: a – Lobbyist: c
Page 70: Onus: a – Precarious: c – Sagacious: a – Trepidation: b
Page 71: Amass: a – Callow: c – Depravity: a – Execrable: a
Page 72: Immoderate: a – Lofty: a – Opaque: a – Precedent: c
Page 73: Sage: b – Trinket: c – Ambiguity: a – Candid: a
Page 74: Deprecate: a – Exegesis: c – Immutable: a – Longevity: b
Page 75: Opulent: a – Precept: a – Salacious: c – Trite: a
Page 76: Ambiguous: a – Candor: b – Deride: a – Exemplary: a
Page 77: Impartial: a – Loquacious: a – Ordain: a – Precinct: a
Page 78: Sallow: a – Trivial: b – Ambivalence: a – Cantankerous: a
Page 79: Derogatory: a – Exemplify: a – Impecunious: b – Lucid: a
Page 80: Ornate: a – Precipice: a – Salubrious: a – Truant: a
Page 81: Ambulatory: a – Capacious: a – Desecrate: a – Exhaustive: c
Page 82: Impious: a – Ludicrous: c – Orthodox: a – Precipitous: a
Page 83: Salutary: b – Truncate: a – Ameliorate: c – Capitulate: a
Page 84: Desecration: a – Exonerates: a – Impoverished: c – Lukewarm: a
Page 85: Ossify: a – Preclude: b – Sanctimonious: c – Tumult: a
Page 86: Amelioration: a – Carping: a – Desist: b – Exorcism: a
Page 87: Impromptu: a – Lummox: a – Ostentatious: a – Precocious: b
Page 88: Sanction: a – Turpitude: a – Amiable: a – Cartographer: a
Page 89: Despondent: a – Expatriate: a – Inadvertent: b – Luscious: a
Page 90: Oust: a – Predecessor: a – Sanguinary: a – Tyro: c
Page 91: Amity: a – Castigate: a – Destitution: c – Expedient: b
Page 92: Incantation: a – Lynch: a – Overt: c – Predicament: a
Page 93: Sanguine: a – Ubiquitous: c – Amorphous: b – Catharsis: a
Page 94: Deter: b – Expedite: a – Incarceration: c – Machinations: a
Page 95: Overwrought: b – Preeminent: a – Sardonic: a – Unalloyed: a
Page 96: Maelstrom: a – Palatable: c – Prerogative: b – Savant: a
Page 97: Unctuous: a – Analogous: c – Caustic: a – Detrimental: a
Page 98: Extol: c – Incipient: a – Magnanimous: c – Palisade: a
Page 99: Prescient: a – Scale: a – Undermined: a – Anarchy: c
Page 100: Cavalcade: a – Devoured: b – Extradite: a – Inclination: a
Page 101: Magnate: b – Palliative: a – Presentiment: b – Scapegoat: a
Page 102: Underscore: a – Anecdote: a – Celerity: c – Dexterous: a
Page 103: Extraneous: a – Incoherent: c – Maladroit: c – Pallid: c
Page 104: Presumptuous: a – Scrupulous: b – Unequivocal: a – Animosity: a
Page 105: Censorious: a – Dichotomy: a – Extrapolate: a – Incongruous: a
Page 106: Malady: c – Palpable: a – Pretentious: a – Scrutinize: a
Page 107: Unfetter: b – Annex: c – Censure: a – Didactic: b
Page 108: Extrinsic: a – Inconsequential: a – Malediction: a – Panacea: b
Page 109: Prevaricate: a – Scuttle: c – Unfrock: b – Vital: a
Page 110: Cerebral: a – Diffident: a – Fallacious: b – Inconspicuous: –
Page 111: Malefactor: a – Paradigm: b – Pristine: b – Seminary: a

SOLUTIONS to THE 750 STORIES

Page 112: Unprecedented: a – Anomaly: a – Certitude: a – Digress: c
Page 113: Falter: a – Indelible: b – Malinger: c – Paradox: a
Page 114: Proclivity: a – Sensuous: b – Unscathed: a – Antagonism: c
Page 115: Charlatan: a – Dike: c – Fanatical: a – Indifferent: a
Page 116: Malingerer: a – Paragon: a – Procrastinate: a – Sentinel: c –
Page 117: Unwitting: c – Antagonistic: a – Chary: a – Dilatory: a
Page 118: Fanaticism: b – Indigenous: c – Malleable: a – Paramount: a
Page 119: Prodigal: a Sequester: c – Upbraid: a – Antediluvian: b
Page 120: Chastises: c – Dilemma: a – Fastidious: b – Indolence: a –
Page 121: Mallet: c – Parasite: b – Prodigious: b – Serendipity: b
Page 122: Uproarious: a – Anthology: a – Chicanery: a – Dilettante: c
Page 123: Fatuous: a – Inductee: b – Manipulatable: a – Parched: a
Page 124: Profane: b – Serene: c – Upshot: a – Anthropocentrism: c
Page 125: Chimerical: b – Diligent: a – Feasible: a – Indulgent: a
Page 126: Marred: c – Pariah: a – Profanity: b – Serrated: a
Page 127: Urbane: b – Antiquated: b – Choleric: a – Diorama: b
Page 128: Fecund: a – Inebriation: a – Marshal: b – Parity: c
Page 129: Profound: a – Servile: a – Usurp: c – Apathetic: b
Page 130: Chronicler: c – Dirge: a – Felicitous: c – Ineffable: a
Page 131: Marsupial: a – Parochial: c – Profundity: a – Skeptical: b
Page 132: Utilitarian: c – Apathy: a – Circuitous: a – Disapprobation: a
Page 133: Fervor: c – Inept: a – Martinet: a – Parody: a
Page 134: Proletarian: c – Skirmish: a – Utopian: c – Apocryphal: b
Page 135: Circumlocution: a – Discern: c – Fickle: a – Inertia: a
Page 136: Masochist: a – Parry: b – Prolific: b – Sluggard: a
Page 137: Vacillate: a – Appease: b – Circumscribe: a – Discord: a
Page 138: Finesse: a – Inevitable: b – Matriarchy: b – Parsimonious: a –
Page 139: Proponents: b – Smelt: a – Vacuous: a – Apprehensive: c
Page 140: Circumspect: b – Discordancy: b – Fitful: c – Inexorable: b
Page 141: Maverick: a – Parsimony: a – Prosaic: b – Smorgasbord: a
Page 142: Vagrant: c – Arable: a – Circumvent: a – Discrepancy: c
Page 143: Flagrant: b – Inexpedient: b – Meager: a – Partisan: a
Page 144: Proscribe: c – Solace: a – Vapid: a – Arbitrary: a
Page 145: Clairvoyant: c – Discriminate: a – Flamboyant: a – Infallible: c
Page 146: Meander: a – Pathos: b – Prosody: a – Solicit: a
Page 147: Variegated: c – Arcane: a – Clamor: a – Discursiveness: a
Page 148: Flaunt: c – Infamous: a – Mellow: c – Patron: a
Page 149: Prostration: b – Somnambulist: a – Vehemence: c – Archaic: b
Page 150: Clandestine: a – Disdain: c – Flippant: a – Infer: b
Page 151: Menagerie: a – Patronize: a – Protagonist: a – Soothsayer: c
Page 152: Vehement:: a – Archetype: a – Clemency: a – Disinterested: c
Page 153: Flout: a – Ingénue: a – Mendacious: a – Paucity: c
Page 154: Protean: b – Sophomoric: b – Venal: b – Archives: a
Page 155: Cliché: b – Disparage: c – Flustered: a – Ingrate: c
Page 156: Mercenary: a – Peccadillo: a – Protégé: b – Soporific: a
Page 157: Veneer: a – Articulate: a – Clientele: a – Disparity: a
Page 158: Fly-by-night: a – Inimical: c – Mercurial: a – Pedant: a
Page 159: Protocol: b – Sparse: b – Venerate: a – Artifice: c
Page 160: Coalesce: a – Dispassionate: a – Forensic: a – Innate: c
Page 161: Merge: b – Pedestrian: a – Provincial: a – Specious: c
Page 162: Venial: c – Artisan: c – Coddle: b – Disseminating: b
Page 163: Fortitude: a – Innocuous: a – Metaphorically: a – Peerless: a
Page 164: Prudent: a – Speckled: a – Veracity: b – Ascetic: b

SOLUTIONS to THE 750 STORIES

Page 165: Coercion: a – Diurnal: a – Fortuitous: c – Innovate: b
Page 166: Meticulous: a – Pejorative: a – Puerile: a – Sporadic: a
Page 167: Verbose: a – Assiduous: a – Cogent: b – Divert: a
Page 168: Fractious: b – Inscrutable: a – Mettle: a – Pellucid: a
Page 169: Punctilious: b – Spurious: a – Verbosity: a – Assuage: a
Page 170: Cogitate: a – Docile: c – Fraudulent: a – Insentient: c
Page 171: Milieu: a – Pensive: b – Purloin: a – Stagnant: b
Page 172: Vertigo: a – Astute: c – Collage: a – Dogmatic: a
Page 173: Frivolous: a – Insipid: b – Mire: a – Penury: a
Page 174: Pusillanimous: b – Staid: a – Vestigial: b – Asylum: a
Page 175: Collate: c – Dolt: b – Frugal: a – Instigate: b
Page 176: Misanthrope: c – Perceptive: a – Pyromania: a – Stanza: a
Page 177: Vignette: b – Atheist: a – Colloquial: a – Dotard: a
Page 178: Furrow: b – Instigator: a – Misnomer: a – Percipient: a
Page 179: Quaff: a – Staunch: c – Vilification: c – Atrophy: a
Page 180: Collusion: b – Drawl: a – Furtive: a – Insurgent: a
Page 181: Misogynist: a – Perdition: a – Quagmire: a – Stereotype: a
Page 182: Vindicate: a – Attenuate: b – Commandeer: b – Drivel: b
Page 183: Futile: b – Interminable: a – Misrepresentation: a – Peremptory: a
Page 184: Quaint: c – Stevedore: a – Virtuoso: a – Augment: a
Page 185: Complacent: a – Droll: a – Galleon: b – Intermittent: a
Page 186: Mitigate: b – Perfidy: a – Quandary: c – Stifle: c
Page 187: Virulent: a – Auspicious: c – Compliant: a – Drone: a
Page 188: Gambol: a – Intransigence: b – Modicum: a – Perfunctory: a
Page 189: Quarantine: c – Stoic: a – Annex: a – Analgesic: a
Page 190: Caucus: a – Deteriorate: a – Exposition: c – Incessant: a
Page 191: Alacrity: a – Burgeon: c – Deleterious: a – Euphemism: a
Page 192: Hypocritical: c – Lethargic: a – Ogle: c – Postulate: b
Page 193: Robust: a – Tractable: c

LEARN BETTER, LEARN FASTER
SAT STRATEGY
Through **SHORT STORIES**
- Vol. 1 -

How to Efficiently Use Your SAT Prep 2024 – 2025 Vocabulary Builder Vol. 1
- Experience a Narrative-Based Learning Journey for Better Memory Retention -

Unlock the power of immersive storytelling to perfect your SAT preparation. This unique approach integrates 750 of the most frequently occurring SAT words into captivating short stories and narratives, designed to amplify your memory retention and comprehension by tenfold.

1. Immerse Yourself in Short Stories

Dive into a few narratives each day. Visualize the content as it unfolds, allowing the repeated exposure to vocabulary within these contextual stories to significantly enhance your memorization and understanding. Encountering a blend of familiar and new words throughout these stories reinforces your vocabulary foundation, preparing you for the actual SAT test experience.

2. Active Recall and Practical Application

Challenge your memory by actively recalling these short stories and integrating the vocabulary within them. Use the words in sentences and potentially discussions. This method solidifies your comprehension and makes memorization more dynamic and effective.

This technique mirrors the contextual understanding required during your actual SAT test, ensuring each story enhances retention and comprehension, making your learning process both efficient and enjoyable.

The power of assimilating vocabulary through stories and active recall is undeniable.

Also included are additional synonyms for the 750 SAT vocabulary words featured. This method ensures a thorough and comprehensive grasp of the SAT vocabulary, equipping you with the necessary skills for the test.

Take control of your SAT preparation with a personalized approach. Master the vocabulary that will set you apart and boost your confidence.

I wish you great success in your upcoming SAT!

LEARN BETTER, LEARN FASTER
SAT STRATEGY
Through SHORT STORIES
- Vol. 1 -

The Essential SAT 2024 - 2025 Vocabulary Builder Vol.1
Learning Through Short Stories.

A Revolutionary Approach to Mastering SAT Words.

Welcome to your **SAT Preparation 2024-2025 Vocabulary Builder**, a groundbreaking volume designed to transform your SAT preparation experience through the art of storytelling. This book integrates 750 of the most challenging and advanced SAT words into captivating short stories. This unique method ensures that you not only learn but also retain and comprehend these essential vocabulary words, all through the immersive experience of narrative-based learning.

The Power of Storytelling in Learning
Storytelling is one of the oldest and most effective ways to convey information and instill knowledge. From ancient myths to modern novels, stories have always been a powerful tool for teaching, engaging the mind, and fostering understanding. Our brain is wired to remember stories far better than isolated facts or lists. By integrating your SAT vocabulary into engaging narratives, you utilize the natural human inclination for storytelling to boost your learning experience.

Why Short Stories?
Short stories offer the perfect medium for this innovative learning approach. They are concise yet rich in context, providing just enough content to introduce and reinforce new vocabulary without overwhelming you the reader. Each story in this book is carefully crafted to include SAT words in various contexts, making it easier for you to grasp their meanings and nuances. This method not only helps in memorizing words but also in understanding how they are used in different scenarios, which is crucial for excelling in the SAT.

Immersion and Repetition for Better Retention
Our approach is based on the principles of immersion and repetition. By immersing yourself in a new story (or a few) every day, you encounter SAT words repeatedly in various contexts, which significantly enhances memorization. The stories are designed to be engaging and memorable, ensuring that the vocabulary sticks with you long after you've finished reading. This repeated exposure is key to building a robust vocabulary foundation that will serve you well on test day and after.

Active Learning Through Contextual Understanding
Words need context to come alive, and that's exactly what our short stories provide. Understanding words in different contexts helps you grasp their nuances and subtleties. This method not only prepares you for the SAT but also enhances your overall language skills.

LEARN BETTER, LEARN FASTER
SAT STRATEGY
Through SHORT STORIES
- Vol. 1 -

Active Recall and Practical Application
Challenge your memory by actively recalling these short stories and integrating the vocabulary within them. Use the words in sentences and potentially discussions. This method solidifies your comprehension and makes memorization more dynamic and effective. This technique mirrors the contextual understanding required during your actual SAT test, ensuring each story enhances retention and comprehension, making your learning process both efficient and enjoyable.

A Personalized Learning Journey
Everyone learns differently, and your book is designed to accommodate this. You can go through the stories at your own pace, focusing more on the words and stories that you find challenging. This personalized approach ensures that your study time is effective and tailored to your individual needs. By taking control of your learning journey, you can maximize your preparation and boost your confidence for the SAT.

Comprehensive Solutions and Synonyms
This book also provides thorough solutions for each story, and for the 750 SAT vocabulary words included, three additional synonyms are provided. This approach ensures a broader vocabulary base and a more nuanced understanding of each word. It gives you an edge in the SAT test and well beyond.

Why This Book is Essential for Your SAT Preparation?
The SAT is not just a test of knowledge; it's a test of critical thinking and comprehension. A strong vocabulary is essential for achieving a high score, whatever the SAT disciplines you are taking, and offers a unique and effective way to build that vocabulary. By integrating learning into the enjoyable activity of reading short stories, we make the process less tedious and more engaging. This not only helps in retaining the words but also in understanding their practical applications.

The **SAT Preparation 2024-2025 Vocabulary Builder Vol. 1** is more than just a study guide; it's a comprehensive tool designed to transform your SAT preparation. By combining the power of storytelling with the principles of effective learning, it offers a unique approach that ensures you not only learn but truly master the SAT. This book is your key to unlocking a higher SAT score and achieving your academic goals.

Take control of your SAT preparation today. Dive into the world of short stories, immerse yourself in captivating narratives, and watch your vocabulary and comprehension skills soar.

With SAT Preparation 2024-2025 Vocabulary Builder, you're not just preparing for a test; you're setting yourself up for success in your academic journey and beyond.

LEARN BETTER, LEARN FASTER
SAT STRATEGY
Through SHORT STORIES
- Vol. 1 -

TOP 7 Key Advantages of Learning Through Short Stories in Building our SAT Vocabulary Mastery

Reading short stories can be a very very effective strategy for improving your vocabulary and mastering your SAT.

1. Contextual Learning: Short stories provide a rich context that helps you understand how words are used in different situations. This contextual learning can improve retention and comprehension of new vocabulary.

2. Engagement and Interest: Short stories are often engaging and interesting, which can make your learning new words more enjoyable. When you're interested in the content, you're more likely to remember the vocabulary used.

3. Exposure to Diverse Language: Short stories often use a wide range of vocabulary, including less common words and phrases that often appear on the SAT. This diverse language exposure can help build a more robust vocabulary.

4. Repetition in Various Contexts: Words in short stories are often repeated in different contexts, which reinforces learning. Seeing the same word used in multiple ways helps solidify its meaning and usage.

5. Improvement in Reading Comprehension: Regularly reading short stories improves your overall reading comprehension skills. Better comprehension leads to better understanding of vocabulary in context, which is crucial for your SAT reading section as well as all the other sections.

6. Memorable Characters and Plot: The memorable characters and plot lines in short stories can create mental links with specific words. Associating words with stories makes them easier to recall during your exam.

7. Efficient Use of Your Time: Short stories are typically quick reads, making it easy to fit reading and vocabulary learning into a busy schedule. This efficiency is especially useful for students balancing multiple study commitments.

Integrating short stories into your study routine will make your process of building SAT vocabulary more effective and enjoyable than ever.

In 5 words: The Power of Short Stories. Use it to build today your SAT Vocabulary Mastery and more, as you develop other skills!

About The Author

Dex Saunier holds a Bachelor of Science in International Management, an IELTS, TOEFL, and TEFL certifications, and regularly embarks on a journey of relentless learning of new skills. He regularly help young adults to master and ace their SAT test, though critical thinking and training.

Dex Saunier is as well an entrepreneur, an executive coach to hands-on owners and management teams, a business adviser, and involved in career and startup coaching. He is a passionate public speaker on leadership and communication topics. His work has helped hundreds become better leaders, communicators, and influencers in their fields.

During his journey towards innovation, he developed a keen interest in the evolution of visual learning, critical thinking, decision-making, and problem-solving skills as a mean to develop further soft skills. He has also published several book series, flowing from his passion for creating content from scratch and publishing.

He has lived in Paris, London, and Hong Kong and currently resides in Shanghai. He has two incredible awesome daughters.

Today, he continues to coach youngsters and adults, create workshops and deliver keynote speeches. To stimulate the mind's activity, he regularly releases original books for everyone to enjoy and challenge themselves.

THANK YOU AGAIN

**For Additional Books
Visit Dex Saunier on Amazon**

MY NOTES

Made in the USA
Las Vegas, NV
21 October 2024

10068775R00122